Successful Project Management in Social Work and Social Care

C000094065

Essential Skills for Social Work and Social Care Managers
Edited by Trish Hafford-Letchfield

Excellent management skills are an essential part of delivering services and play a key role in successful outcomes for service users. This series features short, accessible guides to the essential and everyday management skills involved in social work and social care management. The books consider the business aspects of management whilst retaining a focus on ethical practice, and include reader exercises, practical tools and useful frameworks.

Trish Hafford-Letchfield is Senior Lecturer in Social Work and Teaching Fellow, Interprofessional Learning at Middlesex University, UK.

other books in the series

How to Become a Better Manager
Essential Skills for Managing Care
Les Gallop and Trish Hafford-Letchfield
ISBN 978 1 84905 206 1
eISBN 978 0 85700 442 0

Successful Project Management in Social Work and Social Care

Managing Resources, Assessing Risks and Measuring Outcomes

Gary Spolander and Linda Martin

Jessica Kingsley *Publishers*
London and Philadelphia

Table 5.4 on p.92 from European Commission 2004 is adapted
with permission from the European Commission

First published in 2012
by Jessica Kingsley Publishers
116 Pentonville Road
London N1 9JB, UK
and
400 Market Street, Suite 400
Philadelphia, PA 19106, USA

www.jkp.com

Library of Congress Cataloging in Publication Data
A CIP catalog record for this book is available from the Library of Congress

British Library Cataloguing in Publication Data
A CIP catalogue record for this book is available from the British Library

ISBN 978 1 84905 219 1
eISBN 978 0 85700 460 4

Printed and bound in Great Britain

This book is dedicated to our families who have encouraged, supported and coped with the long hours, angst and writing. Thank you, Gail, Terry, Keelan and Luke.

Contents

Figures, Tables and Boxes

Series Editor's Foreword

This book acknowledges the specific need for social work and social care managers to develop essential knowledge and skills required to manage a wide portfolio of projects in a very demanding context. In the UK and internationally, the face of public services has changed dramatically in the last three decades, not only as a result of political ideologies and the fast-moving government policies that impact on provision, but also in the wake of a severe financial crisis and two major world recessions.

The introduction of market-like mechanisms to the provision of services and broad policy themes such as affordability, fairness, intergenerational justice, social mobility, increased choice and personalization of care have inevitably influenced the way in which managers in social work and social care organizations conduct their everyday business. Managers need to develop a more comprehensive and detailed understanding of the challenges and opportunities facing them, alongside creativity and the willingness to consider more radical approaches and solutions.

For some time now, the abilities and requirements of managers to be able to work in partnership with other agencies across sectors and disciplines, in a competitive and complex environment, have been our bread and butter, but there is still a long way to go. In many of these scenarios, social work and social care have taken a leadership role in establishing shared approaches and in developing the capacity for achieving sustainable change to address a range of complex social problems. Adopting project approaches and managing a more outcome-based approach to the development of services have demanded that we develop some new and unfamiliar skills, but the core values of social work and social care remain unchanged and continue to have enduring relevance within project management. Principles of promoting participation and adopting a more distributory style of leadership, and focus on citizenship and identifying and building on the strengths of individuals and their communities alongside promotion of equality and diversity, have underpinned the authors' approach to this book.

There are a number of quality texts on project management, but within this particular text Spolander and Martin have sought to make these more accessible and relevant to the specific needs of social work and social care. For example, the book is underpinned by real-life case studies of project management at different levels and in different settings which are used as a basis to explore the different issues involved. Likewise, the topics addressed in each chapter document the unfolding journey of a project and how this is typically managed by highlighting good practice and providing pointers for adopting a range of techniques and skills relevant to everyday practice.

This book is the second in the series *Essential Skills for Managing Care* which is aimed at front-line or aspiring managers and seeks to provide a practical quality guide to project management skills. Books in the series have been particularly tailored for those working in social work and social care environments or any environment which has care at the core of its business.

The style of the book aims to be informal but draws on a sound knowledge base. Common features include:

- Setting out the broader context for the skill being considered, including a summary of the knowledge base and any relevant research findings.

- 'On the Spot' activities which encourage reflection on the skill being discussed.

- Explaining practical tools that can be used in project management, demonstrated through direct application to a familiar case study.

- A summary and action checklist for each area of skills discussed.

Each chapter is underpinned by the values and ethics of good management in social work and social care, drawing on the principles of distributed and participatory leadership. Project management is a practical activity and involves a continuous process of adaptation to changing pressures and opportunities in a complex political environment. There is a danger of overemphasizing technical knowledge and skills and dependency on which specialist areas of practice and knowledge are prioritized. We also need to keep our eye on the broader structural issues, and this book aims to make sense of these through its frequent references to the personal and democratic elements of project management. These are essential to retain the professional nature of the work in social work and social care and the values inherent in practice. Individual chapter topics include:

- An introduction to project management, what it is and what it isn't, defining how project management differs from other strategic and operational management roles.

- Examples of three real-life projects in action which illustrate some of the different forms projects can take in terms of their subject, purpose, scale and approach. These demonstrate that project management can be useful across a wide spectrum of work and also provide an illustrative basis for discussing the different stages in the following chapters.

- The context for project management in relation to managing change, discussing some of the issues around selecting projects and setting out the frameworks for successful management.

- A reflection on stakeholders' experience of projects undertaken within social work and social care through the narratives of two service users who have been actively engaged in projects, as well as the perspective of an NHS stakeholder. These narratives provide a useful staging post for reflecting on how we undertake projects and the impact it has on those who we engage and design services for.

- The project management process through an examination of the project life cycle from beginning to end and as a process for managing change.

- Leadership skills in managing projects and adapting one's own leadership style to projects one is responsible for.

- Exploring risk in relation to project management, including identifying risk factors, mapping and analysing project risks, developing strategies to prevent risk and using project approaches to promote service improvements.

- Ending projects and the importance and contribution of governance to project management, including illustrating structures for controlling and reporting on project outcomes.

- The diverse and cultural dimensions of project management and the knowledge and skills required to manage projects successfully across diverse cultures.

Project management is often something we learn through experience and through the challenges we face in engaging with our partners and stakeholders necessary to achieve the wellbeing of whole populations. By working through the different topics discussed by Spolander and Martin and their contributors, I hope that readers will get a real feel for the dynamics of the way we approach change and some of the practical tools that can be used to engage successfully with the reality of those potentially affected by our work. I hope you enjoy the challenge.

Trish Hafford-Letchfield
Series Editor

Acknowledgements

We would like to thank our co-contributors for their time and input. Our special thanks to our editor, Trish Hafford-Letchfield, for your patience, encouragement and faith. Thanks to Lambert Engelbrecht for his reflection on the cultural aspects of project management. We are grateful to those co-contributors who shared their professional and personal knowledge and practice experience to bring the chapters to life, particularly Deborah Hadwin, Fiona Metcalfe, Claire Old, Lorraine Stanforth, Rashida Suleman and Colin Tysall.

We are grateful to those who have granted us permission to reprint valuable materials. Every effort has been made to acknowledge sources of this work. Any notifications of omissions or errors in acknowledgements in this work will be gratefully received.

Chapter 1

Introduction to Project Management

Introduction

This book seeks to provide a practical and practice guide to social work and social care professionals on project management. The role of project manager is often different from other roles that you might be involved in as part of your work, and as you work through this book, you may reconsider what this role is. We hope that the book will therefore challenge you to consider the extent of differences in activity, and reflect on the tools used and how these might influence or help you to ensure good and effective services.

The book has been written with recognition that people have a wide range of experience and knowledge in project management and that by helping to demystify the process and facilitate practitioners' knowledge and experience then you may feel more confident in managing projects. As a result, we provide relatively short and straightforward chapters that explain principles and apply those principles to the social work and social care sector. The book provides an opportunity to reflect on the experiences of those managers and professionals who have been involved in projects, and aims to facilitate and consolidate the development of your own project management skills.

This chapter will start by identifying what we mean when we talk about project management and will provide an explanation of the differences between projects and operations management, which should help to clarify when and why project management techniques should be used. One of the key issues discussed in this chapter is the use of projects in promoting change, and the challenges this brings. We shall finish by looking at these challenges in a more positive light, for example by identifying what factors enable and facilitate project success.

Project management in social work and social care

Prior to the Second World War, social care was largely provided under the auspices of Poor Law, which provided the only public-funded care for older and physically disabled people (Thane 2009). Following the establishment of the welfare state in 1948 all health services were 'free at the point of delivery' and local authorities became responsible for social care.

Before 1979 the ideas of 'performance' and 'management' were seldom heard and were mostly associated with the business world. State welfare services were largely provided through 'bureau-professional regimes' through social services departments which were established following the Seebohm Report in 1968 (Harris and Unwin 2009, p.9). Bureau-professional regimes were concerned with ensuring impartiality, enabling professional discretion and ensuring that legal requirements were met. The rise of neoliberalism and new public management resulted in changes to the control of professions, increased use of the private sector (Hafford-Letchfield 2007) and a greater emphasis on learning from the business sector about how to provide public services.

This chapter considers this specific context and seeks to explore the role of project management within the unique circumstances of social work and social care. It draws on a successful methodology widely used in business and the public sector to undertake change and deliver projects, and seeks to apply this within the social work and social care sector. In doing so, we will be making use of case examples to illustrate both methodology and tools. As there are very few case studies that can illustrate all the complexity and aspects of a project, in this book we have sought to use multiple case studies. Chapters 2 and 4 specifically speak from the voices and experiences of those actually involved in delivering projects, and we seek to link these case vignettes to the principles and tools explored so that you have the opportunity to consider the direct application of project management in social work and social care. These case studies have not been edited but illustrate some of the practical realities by enabling those in the case studies to tell their own story.

What is project management?

Project management is the process of managing a project, and whilst the nature of projects and the areas in which they are undertaken may vary, the process of delivering them is largely similar. Projects are work activities that are undertaken within organizations to produce outcomes, and will have a defined start and a clear end. Examples of projects that you are likely to have come across may include:

- changing the culture of care
- undertaking research or audit (Marshall and Hughes 2008)
- development of new services or the decommissioning of old services
- installation and implementation of new technology, for example IT systems
- changes to the supply chain for care, for example outsourcing of goods and services to external providers of those services
- outsourcing of key processes involved in delivering care such as training, finance and human resource management
- ensuring that best practice is implemented throughout care services and facilities
- commissioning and construction of new buildings
- changing protocols used in the provision of care to service users.

There are a number of different methodologies that are used in managing projects and there is a range of literature on general project management (Charvat 2003). However, there appears to be significantly less work published on project management applied to social work and social care. One key framework used for project management within the UK is the PRINCE2 methodology. This is a highly structured approach, which uses a standardized methodology and is used in many large corporations, as well as the UK government. It relies on a well-structured and documented approach (OGC 2011) which:

- demands clarity on the business rationale for the project
- supports structured approaches to project management
- identifies the 'product' the project is delivering
- specifies which stages and processes can be controlled
- proposes methodology to be applied at different levels of the project.

Many of these attributes will be discussed in this book in order to support your knowledge development in project management.

The differences between project and operational management

You will notice that projects are clearly different from what might be termed 'operations' and that all organizations may undertake either or both of these functions. In thinking about the differences, by 'operations' we mean activities that are ongoing, perhaps even repetitive, and that might be considered part of the day-to-day functioning of an organization. These 'operations' are not one-off but are routine activities. Examples here might include:

- ongoing delivery of care services

- the assessment and review of support services provided to service users and carers

- undertaking financial assessments and the processing of the administration linked to this.

To help explain the difference, Table 1.1 illustrates some of the key differences that might be evident between operations and projects.

An example of a project might include the implementation of a new records management IT system in a large social work or social care agency setting. The new system is seen as a way to support front-line practice, improve standards and consistency, improve care quality, reduce the burden of performance management data collection and decision-making, and increase cost savings. In this example the organization believes that front-line practice can be improved through greater use of standardized practice, automated generation of documentation for funding and care decisions, and making information more widely available for all workers dealing with a service user or carer. This consistency is seen as contributing to and therefore improving the quality of care (Munro 2011). Information would be used to support service planning and delivery, and reduce duplication for users, families and workers. Their initial calculations suggest that this will result in improved efficiency, less time for administration and reduced duplication. Management savings would result from improved data collection, reduced administrative duplication and effective use of information.

Table 1.1 A comparison between operations and projects

	Operations	Projects
Features	Planned, implemented and managed, normally involving resource constraints	Planned, implemented and managed, normally involving resource constraints
Function	Maintain and grow organization	Achieve objectives and then end the project
Time requirements	Ongoing processes	Limited timescales. Clear start and end
Product	Achieve specified goal	Ongoing provision of services, products
Human resources	Teams are normally aligned to organizational structures	Teams are generally more dynamic and made up of people with the necessary skills to complete the project. Not normally aligned to organizational structures
Manager's role	Direct and formal lines of accountability	Varies, but normally the line manager has no direct role

The project is complex, as a result of the significant change required:

- Changes to software and training are required to operate the new system.

- Computer hardware changes might be required as a result of the new software requirements.

- Computer networks need upgrading as a result of the new hardware and software demands, but also the operational teams are geographically dispersed.

- New software and standardization of processes requires review, negotiation and adjustments to be made to work processes and software. This may require understanding of the work and professional practice, analysis, development of models to replicate this, debate, and negotiation to ensure that professional, service user and organizational needs and requirements are met.

- Procurement of all the necessary equipment and support staff is required. This may involve the development and issuing of tenders, followed by evaluation and successful 'letting'.

- Pilots of revised practice models, software, hardware and networks need to be undertaken, and adjustments and changes made as appropriate.

- Accuracy of data on existing systems must be checked, and protocols developed and checked to support data transfer from the old legacy system to the new software.

- Staff need to be trained to use the new systems.

- The new system needs to be rolled out and a 'go-live' date agreed.

- Data must be transferred from the legacy system, with contingency plans in place in case of problems.

- Once fully implemented, the old system needs to be removed and surplus equipment disposed of.

Whilst this example is of a large project, it has been used to illustrate the complexity and interrelationships between different aspects of the project. You will recognize that this project is far wider than what initially might be viewed as a change of software. In project management this is often the case.

Table 1.1 showed that projects differ from day-to-day operations in a number of key areas, including being focused on their task, the time frames and resourcing. A project may be a single initiative that is being undertaken in isolation. It is important to note that often the organizational line manager may have no direct role in managing the project manager. The project process is often very formalized, with documentation supporting all the processes, to help ensure that everything that is important is dealt with. Keeping formal records which document the process, although time-consuming, is viewed as critical in project management regardless of the framework you use, as it helps ensure clarity, transparency, accountability and quality in delivery. Chapter 8 further explores the role of project governance in more detail and the importance of this documentation.

A number of different terms are used to refer to project management. 'Programme management' involves a number of interrelated projects which may have a number of interdependencies. 'Business programme management' refers to a number of programmes and projects all being undertaken simultaneously. The management and skills required to manage each of these successfully may vary considerably in magnitude.

The 'On the Spot' activity in Box 1.1 is aimed at enabling you to start to consolidate your existing knowledge and understanding, help you clarify the differences and begin to ease you into using these management activities. It may be difficult to identify absolute differences between some aspects of projects and operations in social work and social care, for instance if the product is similar in both approaches. We hope that this activity will help you to place yourself in the shoes of a project manager, particularly as you approach the remainder of the book.

Box 1.1

'On the Spot' – Project or operational management?

1. Identify in your own workplace activities that you might consider are 'operations' and those that are 'project' management.

2. Using the points you have identified, write down your rationale for each of the points you have identified.

3. Are there any points that you feel might be debatable? Reflect on the reasons for this.

Project management in context

All organizations and services have challenges in the way they work or the services that they deliver. Importantly, the social work and social care contexts in which projects are undertaken often seek to improve the efficiency, structure, process, quality or extent of services in the sector. Key criteria within which the project needs to be delivered and what might influence its success are important aspects that the project manager needs to be mindful of, including:

- understanding the political context
- who the key stakeholders are (this includes service users, professionals and other agencies)
- clarity about the purpose of the project
- project-critical success criteria and timescales
- the resources available.

The role of project manager can be challenging but also fruitful, and the use of project management tools and techniques can help support the changes being sought. Some who have not used project methodology might define it as 'the art of creating the illusion that any outcome is the result of a series of predetermined, deliberate acts when, in fact, it was dumb luck' (Kerzner 2009, p.4). This is an interesting point as sometimes people claim to be making use of project management methodology when they are actually making use of a haphazard series of tools and techniques which are not being applied systematically. This would be considered by experienced project managers as very risky.

A clear challenge within social work and social care is that project expectations and requirements might from time to time be fluid and change as a result of government or regulatory requirements, evidence from research or best practice, or following service user or professional recommendations. These can pose challenges for project managers who have responsibility to deliver a project to an agreed cost and specified outcomes. Project managers must therefore understand which changes may need to be made, but that increasing the number of changes made make it less likely that the project will be delivered efficiently, effectively and even successfully. It goes without saying that continuing to proceed with delivering a project when the outcomes do not meet the project's regulatory, best practice or original requirements would be costly, a waste of valuable resources and possibly even have ethical and moral considerations. Given the risks that this poses both to projects and those seeking to deliver them, Chapter 7 will go on to explore ways that this can be managed, although if changes are significant it may be necessary to consider whether the project should continue.

Why use project management?

Social work and social care organizations, whether in the public or independent sector, are often required to improve performance with fewer resources (Evans, Hills and Orme 2011). As a result they are constantly being asked to be more productive and efficient and respond to an ever-changing environment, and consequently are under pressure to innovate. Project management is one of the tools that we can use to try to meet these challenges as the methodology offers the opportunity to:

- provide a controlled and useful structure and process to respond to the environment they operate in

- utilize the creativity and innovation available in the organization by focusing efforts and communication on a specific issue for a limited period of time

- use resources as effectively and efficiently as possible to manage change
- engage with stakeholders to gain acceptance of change
- provide a clear structure and information to support management decision-making
- help the organization to be more 'efficient' by ending poorly performing projects earlier rather than waiting for them to come to their natural end.

Theoretically, the benefits of project management do not only accrue for the organization or service, but those involved in project management might also benefit personally from the use of this methodology as it:

- enables the individual to ensure that their skills and expertise are used appropriately for the improvement of services within an organization
- enables the individual to clearly demonstrate their own skills and development as part of their career development
- provides a range of challenges and opportunities, leading the person to demonstrate leadership and actively be engaged in developments
- offers the individual an opportunity to influence the future direction of the service or organization.

The challenges of innovation

From your own experience and from your reading of this chapter so far, you may be aware of the challenges and difficulties of delivering a successful project:

- Most projects have multiple stakeholders, each of whom may have their own needs and expectations of what the project might deliver.
- Each project is unique.
- Often the project team has been assembled to work together for the first time and the project may involve new technologies or new service processes. The team may be drawn from a range of stakeholders, who need to learn to work together and understand differing perspectives on common issues. The project manager may play a critical role in facilitating this teamworking and discussion.

- Communication may need to be across internal organizational boundaries and stakeholders, and should include robust governance on the progress of the project.

- There may be competing demands. Projects must be clearly defined with clear deliverables, exacting timescales, approved resourcing and agreed quality levels, and must meet established stakeholders' requirements.

- Projects can involve working across the organization and meeting organizational governance requirements (e.g. for authorization of payments). Financing is a key issue, particularly as in large projects it is likely that funding may extend over financial and budget years and often will require the project manager to ensure that all governance and probity requirements are met.

- Estimating the resources, time and level of work involved in a project is often difficult. This is because each project is unique; the project team may never have worked together and may not have previous project experience. This all increases the risks to successful delivery.

Projects as a way of facilitating change

Projects are increasingly being seen within organizations as a strategic management tool to actively encourage and manage change. This can range from the introduction of new technology to broader process and service changes, for example assistive technology to maintain independence for frail users of services. Whilst project management skills were previously concentrated in industries such as engineering and computing, due to its importance as a strategic management tool, the constant change in the social care sector highlights its importance as well. The ability of staff to manage projects ensures that the organization is more likely to be able to respond quickly to changes in its own service environment.

No organization has a monopoly on good ideas and initiatives, with many of these being generated by their staff, service users or other stakeholders. The challenge for most organizations is to identify which initiatives to progress through investment in order to deliver improvements. If the organizations you work for are anything like the ones that we have, then it is likely that they will:

- not have sufficient resources (time, people, money, management capacity) to undertake all suggested initiatives

- have ideas for projects that may not easily fit with the organization's strategic focus and therefore may divert valuable attention and resources away from the organization's agreed direction of travel.

As a result, for many organizations those projects most likely to be considered and approved for development are likely to:

- link clearly to the strategy of the organization, for example a domiciliary provider deciding to expand its services into a new geographical area or Deborah's project in Chapter 2, in which her agency is seeking to increase the role and extent of volunteers in the delivery of services to unaccompanied children

- demonstrate tangible benefits for service users, staff and the organization

- help to resolve difficulties or gaps identified in the organization's business or service delivery plans, for example recognizing a deficit in staff skills such as infection control or vulnerable adult protection, or the lack of adequate management information.

It is important to recognize that your project may not be the only one being considered, so to maximize the possibility of it being selected you should align it synergetically with other projects. It is also important to be aware of the differences in role between the key architects in a project, namely:

- the *project sponsor*, who is normally concerned with ensuring that the benefits of any project align with the priorities of the organization and who is ultimately responsible for the delivery of the project

- the *project manager*, whose primary focus is on ensuring successful delivery of the project.

You might find it surprising that the project sponsor is the person ultimately responsible for the project; this is because whilst the project manager has day-to-day responsibility for the operation of the project, the project sponsor is a key decision-maker with access to resources and the organization's senior management.

What might a successful project look like?

In describing the success of a project we should be mindful that there is no universal definition of project 'success', or that for some projects the full extent of the success criteria have not been agreed by all stakeholders.

Projects may even be considered a 'success' for political reasons even when all the requirements previously agreed have not been met. Normally, a successful project will have the following characteristics:

- It has been completed on time, achieved all deliverables, stayed within budget and met all the required performance and quality specifications.

- It has met all its goals and outcomes.

- It has met all stakeholders' expectations.

It is important in measuring success that service users, carers and staff are also involved in the measurement of outcomes for success (Mitchell *et al*. 2011). This will be explored in further detail in Chapters 4 and 9. For the purpose of this book, the term 'stakeholder' will include service users, carers, staff and other organizations including public service organizations involved in delivering care.

However, despite our best efforts, sometimes not all projects are seen to be successful. This makes it really important for us to document all the agreements reached about the criteria that will be used to judge success. Outcomes in social work and social care are important, and this is underlined by standards such as the proposed Professional Capabilities Framework (Social Work Reform Board 2010).

When projects fail

In discussing projects and changes within services, we should also recognize that change is difficult and the experience of stakeholders might be of failed previous initiatives. Previous failed initiatives can be damaging to change as stakeholders who had earlier been involved might expect that efforts may result in similar disappointment. It is therefore important for project managers to be aware of the reasons and the context for previous project attempts, if any. For many organizations involved in failed projects the reasons may involve the following factors:

- Not being able to control the change being undertaken. This might be as a result of poor communication and stakeholder engagement, unclear objectives and inappropriate resourcing.

- Lack of clarity on what needs to be done. This may link directly with projects not being embedded in the strategy of the organization or service or the decision-making within the project being unclear.

Projects involve time-limited allocation of resources to deliver a specified change. To be successful it is important to identify the need for this change or improvement, and establish the change and process required to make the change.

Identify what needs improving
Stage 1 – Project planning
We can see from the issues explored so far that for many organizations there are areas that they could improve, whether its their service, systems, processes, structure, technology or people. At the start of any project you will need to identify the improvement or change that needs to be made and why this needs to be undertaken. This would normally be fully documented in a Project Planning Document (PPD) and will be used in discussions with stakeholders to obtain their agreement and commitment to the project. The development of the PPD signifies the organization's initial commitment to invest resources in the change process and that the process has been formally recognized. The benefit of developing the PPD is that it:

- helps to clarify in writing the ideas and starts the process of communicating these ideas

- signifies the start of the project and helps in the development of the Project Initiation Document (PID). The PID helps to inform and establish the agreements, scope and deliverables of the project.

The planning document is normally a brief but clear document which establishes the reasons why the project is necessary, the proposed outcomes from the project, how it fits with current organizational strategy, the benefits, the costs and impact, resources required and any challenges in delivery.

It is important at this stage that any project being considered aligns strongly with the organization's strategy and plans. Failure to do this might mean that the plan will not obtain commitment and agreement to progress to the next stage. An example might be a project to expand preventative emergency hospital admission programmes due to budget allocation reductions. It would also normally be important at this stage to have the support of a senior member of the organization's management who has seen the proposals and agrees with them. This person would normally become the project 'sponsor' and would be involved in ensuring that the senior management team is coordinated around the project, making sure that there are no other plans for a similar organizational project, ensuring that suitable resourcing is available and also seeking to smooth out difficulties as they are encountered in the organization. The project sponsor is likely also to be the person who confirms the project manager in their role, and who would be responsible for the development and approval of the PID.

Stage 2 – Developing the business case

The PPD clearly sets out the business rationale for the project, although at this stage it is not a fully worked-out proposal but has sufficient detail that the project is able to move towards its next stage. As a result the document clearly answers the following:

- Why the project is necessary, including the needs of stakeholders.

- Which options need to be considered to meet the needs identified.

- How the project should be undertaken.

- Who is responsible to ensure it develops beyond an idea.

- What resources are required to make the project happen.

- What the strategic links are between the proposals and the organization's strategy.

It is usual at this stage that a project given the go-ahead by the project sponsor will also assemble appropriate people to be involved in the scoping and delivery of the project. It is this group that then starts to work on the PID.

The 'On the Spot' activity in Box 1.2 helps to identify that positive aspects of a project may include being inclusive, valuing contributions, having sufficient resourcing and having clear and agreed outcomes and responsibilities. Negative aspects may include the opposite of those positive aspects: lack of communication, suffering from poor organization and failing to deliver outcomes. Chapter 4 highlights the experiences of stakeholders who do not feel the project was a true partnership, were disempowered, and suffered from poor communication and attempts to maximize some outcomes at the expense of others.

Box 1.2

'On the Spot' – Exploring perspectives on projects

1. Identify two projects you have experience of, either as a project manager or as a participant.

2. Reflecting on the project, write down the positive and negative aspects of the project from your perspective.

3. Now place yourself in the position of another stakeholder in the project (preferably someone on the receiving end of the change that was undertaken). Considered from their perspective, write down what they may perceive as the positive and negative aspects of the project.

4. Reflect on what might have helped mitigate the challenges and further enhanced the benefits.

Challenges in interdisciplinary and multi-agency environments

Utilizing the dynamic and diverse skills from interdisciplinary and multi-agency environments is necessary to support the effective scoping and planning of projects. This is important as few people in social work and social care have simple needs; most have complex needs involving multiple agencies or multiple disciplines. As a result, engagement with service users, carers, partner agencies and staff is key to understanding the needs of all stakeholders, and this understanding, together with their contributions, is essential to assist efforts to resolve difficulties and preparedness. Examples of this can be found in Performance Inspection Reviews such as that undertaken in Fife (SWIA 2006). By widening planning to include non-traditional planning partners, for example young people, those with complex and multiple needs and minority ethnic groups, it increases access to at-risk and hidden populations which are often difficult to engage in project planning (Danforth *et al.* 2010).

Interdisciplinary and multi-agency perspectives utilize local experience and knowledge, engage with different perspectives, facilitate ownership and decision-making, and enable regular feedback loops to be established and further changes to be based on reviews of experience and best practice evidence (Jenkins and Jones 2007). The use of systems thinking in project management facilitates consideration of the interrelatedness between different aspects of the project, the problem it is seeking to resolve and the other components of a system. As a result it recognizes the interaction, interconnections and co-dependencies of the various aspects of a project. By this we mean that individual components of a project may behave differently when separated from the project compared with when they are included. Thus the success of a project is not dependent on the success of each component part alone, but is also dependent on the relationships between the parts that make up the whole.

Chapter summary

This chapter has provided a number of key concepts for you to start considering when developing your project. Before reading the next chapter it would be useful for you to consider the key skills you have developed and how you might consolidate your skills in this regard. For example, understanding why projects may succeed can help to ensure that you build on this knowledge to support you to manage projects more successfully. In particular you should be clear about the differences between successful project and operations management and what the expectations of a project manager would be in any new project. You should recognize the importance of identifying the rationale for commencing a project as well as the possible challenges in successful delivery. Projects, although challenging for all involved, also offer the opportunity to make a real difference to users of care services, their families, social workers and social care staff, and other stakeholders and the organizations they work in. These opportunities also enable project managers to develop their own skills and expertise, their sense of work satisfaction, and develop their careers for future opportunities.

Action checklist

- Reflect on the purpose of the project and identify how you will know if it has been successful.

- Considering the purpose of the project, identify the problem or change the project resolve.

Chapter 2

Projects in Action

Introduction

In Chapter 1 we gave examples of some of the different forms projects can take. We now introduce three contrasting case studies based on real projects. You will see that the projects vary in terms of their subject, purpose, scale and approach, demonstrating that project management can be useful across a wide spectrum of work. However, you will also note some commonalities. They are unique, 'one-off' pieces of work; they have a clear beginning and projected end. These points were raised in Chapter 1 and their implications will be explored further in Chapter 5, but it is worth reflecting on both the differences and the similarities and the impact these have on the management of the projects as you read through them.

Project contexts

- *Case Study 1 – Fiona*
  Fiona is a workforce development manager employed by a county council in the UK. Her role involves working with staff in both children's and adult services, responding to their development needs and enabling them to access appropriate training. This case study relates to her role within children's services. The work took place in 2009 when she was requested by a senior manager to 'project manage' the development of a series of workshops promoting best practice. The initiative was a response to the impact of the inquiry into the death of Peter Connelly, a 17-month-old child who died in 2007 following sustained abuse by his mother, step-father and the step-father's brother. An external inquiry which concluded the following year heavily criticized the local authority children's services where Peter lived (Ofsted, Health Care Commission and HM Inspectorate of Constabulary 2008). Fiona's workshops were intended to raise morale amongst social workers. The case study represents the first three months of the project.

- *Case Study 2 – Deborah*
  Deborah is the assistant manager of a team within a metropolitan borough council in the UK, whose role is to provide services for unaccompanied child asylum seekers. The team was established in the borough as there is an Asylum Reporting Centre there, resulting in asylum seekers throughout the region making their way to the town. The service is partly funded by the UK Border Agency, which processes asylum applications, because it meets a need which is not the sole responsibility of the county. The team is responsible for arranging appropriate care and accommodation for the children and young people who arrive without a responsible adult. They continue to provide support throughout the transition to adulthood. In 2011 the UK Border Agency announced a 15 per cent cut in the service's budget. Deborah was responsible for identifying how the savings could be made. As a result of consultation with her team a proposal was made to introduce a community scheme which would aim to recruit volunteers to provide some of the support to the service users. This was only one possible option which Deborah needed to assess alongside other approaches to save money. The case study is a summary of the first four months of the project.

- *Case Study 3 – Lorraine*
  Lorraine was engaged by a city borough council to develop a Dignity Strategy for Adult Social Care which she completed in 2011. The project was a response to the UK Dignity in Care campaign launched in November 2006 which highlighted the poor quality of care received by some adult service users. As part of her work she developed a protocol for responding to reported incidents of abuse. The work presented here is part of the completed protocol which is based on a project management approach. As you will see, it demonstrates how project management thinking can be used to provide a structure for an area of work, in this case incident investigation.

So, each of the three case studies came about for a different reason. Fiona's was a small-scale project to boost the morale of workers. Senior management determined a strategic response to a perceived short-term problem and Fiona's project was to develop the practical output to achieve the defined goal. Deborah's project was also relatively small-scale as it affected only one team but had far-reaching consequences as the team provided the service for the whole county. Lorraine's was a strategic response to a situation that could arise anywhere in the county. All three case studies represent a blend of strategic and operational responses but with a different balance in each.

Fiona's and Deborah's case studies are presented in the same format as they illustrate the initial stages of longer-term projects. They focus on scoping and planning and demonstrate some of the questions and considerations that are key in the early phase. As Lorraine's is an extract from a completed piece of work, in order to be able to demonstrate the main facets of the template the case study follows a different format from the other two, focusing on how to apply project management in a given situation.

What to look out for

As you read the other chapters of the book reference will be made to bring you back to the case studies to illustrate particular points. However, there are a number of useful points to make as you read through them now:

- Think about how the projects started. Would you have used project management methodology if asked to respond to these situations? It is easy to react to situations and problems without adopting a particular approach. The case studies illustrate the versatility of project management suggested in Chapter 1 and how it can help to structure a proactive response.

- Think about who needed to be involved and the nature of their involvement in order for the projects to reach a successful conclusion. 'Stakeholders' have already been referred to in Chapter 1 and more attention will be paid to this key aspect of project management in Chapter 6. As social workers we are used to working with other people, but we are also used to being 'case responsible'. Our relationships and style of working with others need to be deliberate in project management and may be different from how we have worked in the past.

- Consider the tools that are used to assist with the work of the projects. Throughout the book a range of tools are suggested for use. Chapter 1 referred to using a Project Planning Document and a Project Initiation Document. Chapter 5 demonstrates the use of a Logframe matrix and a Gantt chart. In Chapter 6 we look at stakeholder mapping and in Chapter 7 risk analysis. These are just a few of the possible tools you might use. In the case studies Fiona uses three different analytical tools: PESTLE, SWOT and Force

Field; while Deborah uses the 7S model and systems approach. A brief explanation of each of these is included in the case study.

Points for consideration

As you read through the case studies consider:

- How often do you use tools or conduct specific exercises in your work to assist in your analysis or planning?

- How do you ensure that you have gathered all of the relevant information and reflected on it before making key decisions in your work?

- Can you think of examples in your experience where you could have used an analytical or planning tool such as the ones used in the case studies?

Case Study 1 – Fiona: Developing 'Best Practice Workshops' within Children's Social Work teams in a local authority

Introduction

In response to the death of Peter Connelly the UK central government set up a Social Work Task Force charged with undertaking a review of the key issues facing front-line social work practice, with a particular emphasis on continuous professional development.

In order to stem a possible tide of sinking morale which can result from prolonged focus on problems and negative aspects of service delivery, the Head of Children's Services in the local authority where Fiona worked asked her to project manage a series of Best Practice Workshops. These were to take place at lunchtimes, enabling staff to look at research dissemination and providing a forum for highlighting good practice.

Process
INITIAL CONSULTATION

Fiona initially held discussions with the head of service, colleagues and service managers within the organization who would be supportive of such an initiative and felt that a purely research orientated and academically based series of seminars might be too narrow a remit to attract a broad range of staff. Instead she suggested a more diffuse set of workshops looking at celebrating and sharing good practice within the organization alongside some research dissemination from external and internal sources, believing this would prove a better fit. This was agreed.

A first workshop was successfully launched, and from this Fiona was keen to identify possible best practice champions to create some 'buy-in' and ownership of the initiative from the practitioner level so that it would become their group rather than something imposed top down.

AGREEING OUTCOMES

The Best Practice Workshops aimed to achieve several different but complementary outcomes:

- celebrating and sharing good work across the authority
- looking at developing research mindedness amongst practitioners to build on their confidence, status and credibility in working in multi-professional settings
- providing dissemination opportunities for researchers
- providing network opportunities for staff and engagement with researchers in a more informal and available forum.

ANALYSIS

A range of analytical tools, described below, were deployed to provide a framework for looking at the internal and external context. This included analysis of the perspective of a selection of key stakeholders, social work practitioners, service users and managers to appraise core themes and issues. These different tools of analysis identified both the factors which would enable the workshops to take place and those that would create barriers.

DRIVERS – UK AND LOCAL CONTEXT

A PESTLE analysis was used to help identify key national and local drivers which would impact on the development of Best Practice Workshops. Analysing the drivers encouraged a whole systems approach to thinking about and resolving any issues.

PESTLE stands for:

- Political factors
- Economic influence
- Sociological trends
- Technological innovations

- Legislative requirements

- Ecological factors.

More recently an optional 'I' for industry analysis has been added, making it a PESTELI analysis. Each of the considerations is fairly self-explanatory, and the analysis is a means of identifying the external factors you will need to be aware of when managing your project or assessing whether your project is an appropriate response to the external environment by considering, for example, the demographic trends, policy directives and political will. The PESTLE analysis is illustrated in Table 2.1.

Table 2.1 PESTLE analysis

PESTLE	National drivers	Local drivers
Political	High-profile child protection cases which have hit the headlines and damaged the professional standing of the social work profession	Annual inspections Performance indicators Endorsements from senior management Developing a 'Knowledge Exchange Partnership' between the local authority and higher education institutions
Economic	Value-for-money target outcomes, performance measures, demands for best practice	Local area agreements – emphasis on value for money and need to drive up social work standards
Social	Service users at the heart of shaping services, with accompanying greater demands/ expectations	Transformation agenda, increase in multi-disciplinary teams – importance of social workers reclaiming their profession
Technological	Rapid technological changes affecting ways of working and communicating	Virtual communities of practice Opportunities to harness Internet and Intranet to share best practice, particularly for hard-pressed managers and practitioners
Legal	Recent UK child protection reviews, e.g. Every Child Matters supported by the Children Act 2004, Laming Review Progress Report (2009)	Same drivers for a statutory agency: Every Child Matters, Lord Laming's Review. Review of roles and tasks of social work
Environment (context within which social work operates)	Changing context of social work Transformation agenda	Need to be better informed drawing on evidence-based practice Endorsements from senior management

The PESTLE analysis demonstrated that running the Best Practice Workshops was in accordance with the environment that social work is operating at both a local and national level. In particular:

- The idea reflects the national importance given to good social work practice and the continual development of social workers.

- It highlights the possibility of using technology to support the workshops.

- It is a reminder that social workers do not work in isolation and that the workshops need to be developed in a way which is in harmony with the multi-professional settings they work within.

Engaging stakeholders

Although the project is a positive attempt to value social workers, celebrate their good work and provide opportunities for learning and development and is in keeping with the national and local context, there are organizational complexities that also need to be considered.

Issues affecting the ability of staff to engage with the Best Practice Workshops centre around three main organizational themes:

- The relentless pace of change driven by new initiatives which may sometimes be greeted with cynicism by battle-worn staff.

- The complexities and volume of work resulting in individual social workers being able to prioritize activities viewed as developmental. The support of managers at all levels of the organization would be necessary to permit social workers to commit to the Best Practice Workshops.

- Accessibility – in a geographically spread authority the location of the Best Practice Workshops could deter or encourage attendance.

PRACTITIONER STAKEHOLDERS (SOCIAL WORKERS)

The prime aim of the workshops is to engage practitioners and improve practice. They seek to minimize barriers to learning such as anxiety, lack of confidence, complacency, workload pressure and lack of team and managerial support for learning, and increase the motivation of staff through encouragement, reward, management support and context of shared values.

A key role for those involved is that of project champion. The champions need to be seen as credible, flexible and motivated to take on the role. Those most likely to be attracted to the notion of being a 'champion' would be the so-called 'early adopters' (Rogers 1995) motivated by personal gain and wanting to get things done, seeing the relevance for themselves and the organization. According to Rogers, early adopters are those who respond to change more quickly and positively, and this is explored further in Chapter 6. Associated with becoming a champion is a notion of power: the ability to drive forward ideas. Whilst having champions can be beneficial, it is important to be mindful that personal self-interest does not get in the way of organizational needs. Change 'assassins' can undermine their work and enthusiasm; these are the people resistant to change and new ways of thinking and working. One solution is to ensure that the champion is rooted in the team and communicates, consults and feeds back to their team and does not become a maverick within the organization.

SENIOR MANAGER STAKEHOLDERS

Ideally this group would be both supporters and participants. As supporters they would sanction and enable staff to attend. The head of service had legitimized attendance as an important part of continuing professional development and saw these workshops as integral. As participants, the Best Practice Workshops should not be seen purely as a forum for practitioners but also for managers.

CUSTOMER STAKEHOLDERS (SERVICE USERS)

Although unaware of their status as stakeholders, as the purpose of the workshops is to improve practice for the benefit of this group, they are indirect stakeholders. Their involvement could take a number of different forms:

- presenting a service user perspective
- involvement in planning some activities
- contributing as participants.

The authenticity and integrity of the workshops will depend on not losing sight of this stakeholder group and working actively towards their engagement and involvement.

STAKEHOLDER SWOT

A SWOT analysis focuses on the Strengths, Weaknesses, Opportunities and Threats presented by a situation. Criticism of this tool has been that it can lead to the production of lists rather than action, but this is dependent to some degree on what you do with the lists. Identification of strengths, weaknesses, opportunities and threats is the first stage of the exercise but the challenge is then to identify ways of minimizing the impact of the weaknesses and threats by managing them appropriately (Johnson, Scholes and Whittington 2005).

The SWOT analysis illustrated in Table 2.2 confirms the wisdom of the thinking underpinning the project and shows the potential for success but also highlights a number of potential difficulties which need to be addressed through engaging stakeholders if the project is to be successful:

- The role of service users – this is unclear and there is a danger that engagement may become tokenistic.

- Consistent support of senior managers – although the project was initiated by them, the analysis highlights some doubts about the sustainability of this support which need to be considered.

- Difficulties for social workers in prioritizing their own needs – the support of operational managers appears to be key to the success of the project.

Change management

Although the Best Practice Workshops were a positive idea put forward to support social workers, the initial analyses have shown that there are potential barriers to their success. Force Field analysis is a useful tool for considering what competing forces are at play that would affect and influence people's commitment to the workshops. Force Field analysis was developed by Lewin (1947) and is a useful tool for managing the process of change. Lewin suggests that we need to identify the factors which are driving change and those which are resistant to it. The drivers may be a combination of external factors such as financial restraints and internal factors such as a new chief executive officer, while the restraints can usually be analysed by using the following four headings:

- Administrative factors – for example procedures which may make change difficult.

- Rewards – what people will lose through the change.

- Satisfaction with the way things are done – the higher this is, the less motivation there will be to change.

- Loyalties to other groups – how the change will affect other working relationships.

Table 2.2 Stakeholder SWOT analysis

Stakeholders	Strengths	Weaknesses	Opportunities	Threats	Themes
Practitioners, social workers and other professionals	Opportunities to network, showcase, share practice Learn from each other, develop new ideas Reflect on what works Hear about recent research Time away from front-line	Demands of job Geographical distance Permission from manager Relevance of subject matter Viewed as a management tool Publicizing events to other professionals, encouraging a multi-disciplinary approach	Learn from each other Raise professional status Develop confidence Develop thinking, knowledge and skills	Time Geographical distance Reluctant manager Luxury Confidence of staff to share Skills of workshop facilitator and skill of engaging everyone to own the agenda	Networking learning New thinking Celebrating Building Confidence Time and workload pressures Agenda must be relevant Good promotion Permission to attend Geographical problems
Senior managers	Bridges a gap between research and practice Enables research dissemination Opportunities to highlight good practice within the local authority	Workshops badly attended Achieve little but a talk shop; no identifiable outputs	Engage practitioners in reflecting and looking at practice	No buy-in from practitioners Time workload pressures	Improves practice Engages practitioners in thinking about their practice and engaging with research Research dissemination
Customers	Possibilities to become stakeholders Practitioners become more interested in evaluation/feedback Encourages inclusive approach Encourages sharing of what works	Difficulty of service users becoming full stakeholders. Stakeholders by proxy – this may be enough? If customers presented, issue of being made equal partners	Are they full stakeholders or not? Can they be?	Meaningful, relevant, not tokenistic	

Lewin argues that once we know the drivers and restraints we need to work at minimizing the restraining forces. This will not only increase the drivers but will clear obstacles and make for a smoother transition. If instead we aim to increase the drivers, we will also increase the resisting factors, resulting in a more painful change process.

To some degree, the Force Field analysis has confirmed factors which Fiona had begun to identify using the PESTLE and SWOT analyses. Here, though, you will see that within the restraining factors she has also identified some structural issues regarding the project – constraints on her own time as project manager and the lack of a budget (Table 2.3).

Had she not adopted a project management approach these issues may not have been identified until they had become problematic. Now, instead she can address them before proceeding onto the next phase of the project.

Table 2.3 Force Field analysis

Driving forces			Restraining forces
Senior management endorsement driving standards up	⟶	⟵	Some local managers not engaged or supportive
Lord Laming's review Development of the Advanced Practitioner role for social workers	⟶	⟵	Workload, time and capacity
Practitioner enthusiasm and motivation	⟶	⟵	Geographical issues
Workforce Development – promoting the learning organization	⟶	⟵	Maintaining this as a workload priority
Key stakeholder engagement	⟶	⟵	Motivation wanes, own workload capacity issues. Lack of budget to support Best Practice Workshops

Action plan

The business case (see Chapter 1), with clearly identified deliverables, had already been made for this project prior to the project manager being approached. Although there was an agreed timeframe there was no clearly defined budget, which posed a realistic threat to the project's success.

In order to progress with the workshops, a project group comprising staff and managers from across the county was formed to consider the questions posed earlier regarding the project. The focus of this group was to:

- agree and be clear about the aims and objectives of the project

- initiate good planning – time, team, activities, resources

- develop good communication

- agree and delegate project actions

- manage, motivate, inform, encourage and enable the project team

- oversee progress; adjust project plans, keep the group on board

- review, evaluate and report on project performance; give praise and thanks to the project team.

As this is an ongoing project we are unable to reflect on its completion.

Case Study 2 – Deborah: A pilot project to develop a volunteer support team to work alongside social workers within a local authority unaccompanied asylum-seeking children's team

Introduction

Deborah is a manager in an unaccompanied asylum-seeking children's team (UASC) which was formed in 2004 following the opening of an immigration centre in the borough. The team supports this group of young people from the day of their arrival, through their time as a looked-after child, until they exit as care leavers at the age of 21 or up to the age of 25 if they are engaged in a programme of education or training (DfE 2010). Although the team is integral to the local authority service provision, it is largely funded by the UK Border Agency, a central government department. During 2010, the way central government calculated the grant changed. As a consequence the team had to make 15 per cent savings during the financial year 2011/12.

The profile shown in Table 2.4 illustrates the rapid growth of the work of the team between 2004 and 2009 and how the public sector cuts have impacted since then. Reducing the budget by a further 15 per cent presented a serious challenge.

Table 2.4 Numerical profile of staff and service users

Year	Young people using the service	Staff
2004	100	7
2009	400	38
2011	350	24

The key outcome of the project was pre-determined, that is to make a 15 per cent budget saving. There was a less clear outcome, which was to achieve this with minimal impact to the quality of service delivered, but at the initiation of the project this had not been specifically defined; as different options were considered, this outcome would need to be explored further in order to assess the least damaging alternative.

Process
INITIAL CONSULTATION
As a result of discussion within the service delivery team, a proposal was made to introduce a community scheme which aimed to recruit volunteers to work alongside social workers to ensure that the young unaccompanied asylum seekers could continue to access services and get the support they need.

This was only one possible response to the presenting problem of making 15 per cent budget cuts, but in order for it to be compared with other possibilities further work needed to be done. Consideration of the detail of who the volunteers might be, what work they would be able to undertake and how they would be supported and managed was necessary in order to assess its viability as a way forward. In order to aid this process Deborah adopted a systems approach, examining how action taken in one area inevitably impacts on another, and used the 7S model (Waterman, Peters and Philips 1980) to demonstrate this. She also attended a service user panel comprising users from a range of services to generate ideas and models of practice which could influence the direction of the project.

ANALYSIS
DRIVERS
The most significant driver is the need to make significant budget cuts. However, there is inevitably a range of possible ways to achieve this, so as each option is appraised the drivers need to be carefully assessed.

THE 7S MODEL

Waterman *et al.* (1980) suggest that there are seven points in an organization which need to be congruous to achieve success:

- Strategy
- Structure
- Systems
- Staff
- Style
- Shared values
- Skills.

This approach is similar to the systems approach (see Chapter 7) as it argues that a change in one 'S' will impact on the others. However, the greater challenge in using the 7S model is to identify how to achieve harmony between all seven S's.

Alignment is essential for sustainable success, so an initial analysis of the proposal using the 7S model was conducted (Table 2.5). As the project was only at an embryonic stage this raised more questions but highlighted considerations that would need to be addressed if the community scheme was pursued:

- Management of the community scheme – the possibility of working in partnership with another social work agency from the voluntary sector with a view to that agency managing the volunteer service needs to be considered.

- The implications for other child care services – if this model provides a quality service for young asylum seekers then why not consider introducing the model for other children in care?

- The implications for service users – at what stage should they be consulted regarding the proposal?

PROJECT CHAMPIONS

The proposal to introduce volunteer workers came from two team members. Ultimately the team manager makes the final decision about what ideas will be supported; however, there is freedom for creative thinking and in some ways this is encouraged not just by the leadership style but by the organization as a whole in terms of appraisal criteria. Skills for Care, formerly

TOPSS, also recognize this creativity (Skills for Care 2004). They state that amongst the assets of a good manager are the ability to empower staff and service users to develop services that people want, including valuing people recognizing and actively developing potential (Hafford-Letchfield 2009) which is congruent with social work ethics and values.

Engaging stakeholders
PRACTITIONER STAKEHOLDERS (SOCIAL WORKERS)

As noted in the previous case study (Fiona's), project champions can be very effective in driving a project forward. However, it is also important to consider whether other team members need to become involved. If they did not have the same levels of motivation and belief in the project, might this have an adverse effect? A similar project to introduce peer mentors within the team had stalled when the lead worker for this project left the team to move to a new work role which meant the momentum was lost. This highlights the dangers associated with project champions. Sometimes they may be pursuing a personal goal rather than one which meets the service user, team or organizational needs. On the other hand they may be completely aligned to those needs but be working in isolation as other team members may be happy to 'let them get on with it' as they are so enthusiastic about the project.

In terms of this project, care needs to be taken to develop a team approach. This is primarily an operational team which is about to evolve into a project team as well (see Chapter 1 for an explanation of the differences). Although different team members may take on different roles within the project, it is essential that they are all engaged with and committed to the project as they will continue to work together as an operational team in the future.

SENIOR MANAGER STAKEHOLDERS

A decision made in one area of practice will affect what happens in another. The management team needed to be clear that embarking on this project was a worthwhile venture that once started would stay on track until completion.

Table 2.5 Analysis using the 7S model

Shared values	Strategy	Skills	Structure	Systems	Staff	Style
Strong commitment to young people using the service	Need clear aims and plan	What skills are needed to run the project?	To be determined by who runs and finances the project	Systems will need to be checked for rigour in safeguarding children	Implications for team dynamics if staff proposing project have key role	Will a different style of working be needed to accommodate volunteers?
Strong commitment to GSCC/social work values	Need clarity regarding the role of the volunteers	What skills do volunteers need?	Could be accommodated within current team structures		Need to learn lessons from peer mentoring programme which collapsed when team members left	Is the change in the best interests of the young people using the service?
Need to explore how volunteers would be viewed by team	Service user involvement – at what stage?	Responsibility for and commitment to training and supervision	Model could be considered in relation to all children in care		If run with voluntary sector, power dynamics will be affected	
Need to explore the political underpinnings of the proposal	Funding – this could be run jointly with a voluntary sector agency	Explore potential of student social workers as volunteers	If collaborative with the voluntary sector, roles of all stakeholders will need to be determined			

CUSTOMER STAKEHOLDERS (SERVICE USERS)

Deborah had access to a panel of service users who meet to consider and give feedback on project proposals. The purpose of the panel is to ensure that the projects take account of service users' needs and experiences at an early stage.

The panel is a diverse group with a wide range of experience of services. A free-flowing sharing of ideas resulted in a further option being generated. The project manager presented the options of either recruiting interested volunteers or of working with a higher education institution to recruit volunteers from a professional qualifying course. Neither of these options was dismissed, but a third option took the form of enabling the young service users to run the volunteering service themselves. The 7S analysis had raised many issues about where service users fit into the project, what the impact would be on them and whether it was in their best interest. While this proposal did not provide instant answers to those questions, it provided an alternative model for consideration that could reduce the managerial hierarchy above them, making them central to decision-making and might provide a more sustainable way forward.

Action plan

This project was just at the inception stage and has followed a very different path from Fiona's case study because of being initiated from within the staff group rather than being determined by senior management.

Although there is a financial imperative to this development, the business case (see Chapter 1) has to be made in order for it to proceed. However, this case study demonstrates the importance of examining the impact on practice of different options first, to ensure that good practice is maintained and there is a clear understanding of how a new development will potentially impact on the service users and the staff team before it is agreed and implemented.

Case Study 3 – Lorraine: Project management for institutional abuse

Introduction

As part of the Dignity in Care campaign launched in the UK in 2006 (DoH 2008), a local authority commissioned a strategy development which included a template for responding to any suspicions of institutional abuse of adults. The strategy recommends that the authority use a project management approach to respond to suspicions. What follows is guidance on how to manage an incident investigation, based on project management methodology.

Process

The project management methodology will follow the PRINCE2 methodology, which was explained in Chapter 1. It has been tested and proved effective in the management of projects and can be adapted to fit the purpose and need.

Seven principles operate in the project management of institutional abuse, as follows:

1. *Continued business justification.* Can we justify people remaining in the home and using resources to make necessary improvements? Equally, is there justification for a Concerns Meeting (an initial meeting to air the suspicions and concerns raised)?

2. *Learn from experience.* There is a means by which previous experience can be utilized and implemented to good effect: lessons are sought, recorded and acted upon throughout the safeguarding process and the life of the project. They will be reviewed and updated at future Concerns Meetings.

3. *Defined roles and responsibilities.* There are agreed roles and responsibilities that will engage the provider, service user and carers, operational, contracts and commissioning services, and partners in Health, Metropolitan Police, Care Quality Commission, and Health and Safety.

4. *Manage by stages.* The investigation (project) is planned, monitored and controlled on a stage-by-stage basis. The safeguarding steps will be implemented at each stage and reviewed at reconvened strategy meetings. This will involve having a high-level plan and individual plans that can be monitored at each stage prior to moving forward.

5. *Management by exception.* Tolerances for each stage will be set out in terms of time, cost, quality, risk, scope and benefit. By placing controls at each stage of the safeguarding process the project will be managed through ensuring that residents remain safe throughout the process.

6. *Focus on the desired outcome.* This will in all cases be that people are in receipt of a safe, high quality service that represents value for

money and meets the ongoing needs of the service user. Quality testing will be the key to assurance that the desired outcome has been met together with the reduction in the number of alerts, serious untoward incidents, serious complaints or contractual concerns.

7. *Tailor to suit the project environment.* Each establishment is different in terms of its size, complexity, capability and risk. A large establishment may have a number of repeated low-risk alerts that need a different management approach from a small home with one high-risk alert.

The decision to project manage is to be made on a firm business case agreed by a project board which comprises representatives from health, police and care services.

ROLES AND RESPONSIBILITIES

- *Project board.* This is the body that will approve and steer the project. This will be multi-agency and rest on partnership, collegial and collaborative working to recommend and reach decisions. The group will delegate work through the project manager and identify the knowledge, skills and experience needed to complete specific actions that will be carried out by work managers as directed by the project manager.

- *Project manager.* The role entails ensuring that targets are met, work is progressed according to plan, evidence is collated and there is effective document control.

- *Work managers.* Throughout the life of the project a number of tasks and actions will be identified. The project manager will supervise the day-to-day actions of the work managers such as undertaking specific investigation of an issue.

- *Document controller.* Throughout the life of the project all documents are to be uploaded and updated by the document controller.

PLANS

The agreed *project plan* will be the high-level plan for all safeguarding to ensure the safety, governance and compliance, and clinical effectiveness referencing, throughout the experience of the resident and their informal network.

Underneath this strategic plan there may be individual plans for the safeguarding of individuals based on their specific needs.

Work plans may be formulated and directed by the project manager in the supervision of the work managers.

The *action plan* will be the key document that the provider draws up to address the concerns raised by the project board. The action plan will be risk-assessed for priority and updated in agreement with the project manager.

Management by stages

The mandate to initiate a project for a 'whole home concerns' meeting will come via a number of sources which in most cases, but not exclusively, will be channelled through health or adult social care.

At the 'initial strategy' meeting roles and responsibilities will be delegated to named individuals. The evidence to date will be reviewed, and what action is needed in terms of fact finding – Stage 1 – will be determined.

The initial strategy meeting will also set up a 'Risk Register' and an 'Issue Register'. The former will focus on risks to residents whilst the latter will focus on the effectiveness of the project management process. Both will be reviewed at the end of the project under 'lessons learnt' so that there is continuous improvement in managing safeguarding.

RISK STRATEGY

The risk strategy addresses the probability of risk and the likely impact of risk on the safety of service users.

The purpose of the strategy is to agree the level of acceptable risk. In this instance the major decision to make is: when is it unsafe for people to remain in an establishment, and what are the risks of moving people to an alternative placement? A major inhibiting factor in achieving good outcomes for people is where there exists a fear of putting the organization at risk, both financially and in terms of public relations, reputation or breach of the law. The strategy will need to acknowledge that there will often be some risk, and that trying to remove it altogether can outweigh the quality of life benefits for service users while continuing existing arrangements for safeguarding people. Balance and proportionality are vital considerations in encouraging responsible decision-making. Reasonable risk is about striking a balance and exploring each issue in context. A good approach to risk within the framework of safeguarding is to base risks on human rights, and it is important that the needs of service users are paramount in deciding the level of acceptable risk.

For each of the concerns/issues a risk matrix will be drawn up and kept on the Risk Register. The Risk Register will be updated by the project manager throughout the life of the project.

QUALITY ASSURANCE STRATEGY

The strategy will focus on meeting business expectations as set out in the Dignity Strategy and enabling the desired benefits of these standards to be experienced by service users.

COMMUNICATION STRATEGY

The communication strategy addresses both internal and external communications. It details how the project manager will send information to and receive information from the wider organizations involved with or affected by the project.

ONGOING COMMUNICATION TO PROJECT MEMBERS

- The *Highlight report* should log information on the effectiveness of the project management approach.

- *Exception reports.* If any new risks or issues are identified (or existing ones have changed), update the Risk and Issue Registers.

The stage boundaries are as follows.

STAGE 1 – FACT FINDING

The project manager will coordinate the work plans for each of the work managers, ensuring that the objectives of Stage 1 as identified by the project board are completed. At the end of each stage the project manager will reconvene the Concerns Meeting. At the beginning of each stage a review of the concerns, risks and evidence will be assessed via a comprehensive summary of the Exception and Highlight reports. If it is found that there is a case to answer, the reconvened strategy meeting will commence Stage 2.

STAGE 2 – ACTION PLANNING

In the event that the local authority remains the lead agency to take further action, the next stage will be greater engagement with the provider. Two members of the project board, one of whom is the Chair and the other from commissioning/procurement/contracts, will meet with the provider to formally outline the concerns.

The project manager will throughout this stage meet on a regular basis with the provider to collate information.

STAGE 3 – QUALITY ASSURANCE

The quality assurance stage is led by the senior user from the operational service that the concerns focus on, supported by the Dignity Champion or Dignity Manager. The project manager will in the first instance note on the action plan that evidence has been received to meet the specific action point. The quality assurance group will be supported by a member of the safeguarding service. The document controller will open up an evidence folder and update the action plan as each task is completed.

When all high-risk actions are complete and medium and lower risk actions are in progress the project manager will reconvene a further strategy meeting.

STAGE 4 – CLOSING DOWN THE PROJECT

Before closure of the project can be recommended, the project manager must ensure that the expected results have all been achieved and delivered. The project manager will cross-reference the action plan and quality assurance evidence folder and risk-assess the impact on service users of any outstanding tasks.

STAGE 5 – ORGANIZATIONAL LEARNING

The Central Safeguarding Service will convene a learning meeting which the provider will also be invited to. The aim of the meeting is to establish what went well and what could be helpful to inform any future project and what might have been done differently. The project manager will present the Issue Register and Risk Register and update the Learning Log accordingly.

Chapter summary

The three case studies give a flavour of the range of work that meets the criteria of being a project and can make use of a project management approach.

Fiona's and Deborah's projects show how projects can emerge from various parts of the organization and do not necessarily present themselves neatly as projects with agreed outcomes, a budget or a project team. They also demonstrate how analytical tools can be used to ensure that all relevant information is taken into account and used to highlight the strengths and positives of a project as well as the potential problems and areas which need more exploration. Lorraine's work shows how it is possible to develop an approach to an area of practice which utilizes project management. Her protocol ensures that each investigation will be conducted in a manner that promotes the wellbeing of service users, taking account of their holistic needs while also recognizing the responsibilities of the organization to maintain services and manage risks appropriately. In the next chapter we consider how to manage a project from beginning to end and will refer back to the case studies to illustrate some of the points being made.

Action checklist

- Consider the work you are involved in and identify which could be approached as projects.

- Identify from the agreed outcomes both the strategic and operational issues that the work is addressing.

- Review the tools introduced in this chapter: PESTLE analysis, SWOT analysis, Force Field analysis and the 7S model – and reflect on whether they might be useful in your own project work.

Chapter 3

The Context for Project Management

Introduction

This chapter seeks to explore further the context in which many projects are undertaken in social work and social care. We started to explore some of these ideas in Chapter 1 and will now look at these in more detail by encouraging you to link these to your own project, service and organization. This should focus your thinking on the process through which proposed projects might be selected. A key challenge for any organization is in the management of change. These challenges or difficulties can relate to any or all aspects of managing technology, people, resources, systems, processes, structure or outcomes. Additionally, many organizations have problems in ensuring that the promised benefits are achieved, and we can therefore safely assume that many continue to have difficulty in either managing or controlling change. These challenges are not confined to large-scale changes (e.g. development of a new residential facility) alone, but might also relate to individual objectives or smaller projects such as the review of eligibility criteria.

Project failures can result in substantial costs to the organization, impact negatively on the reputation of all the organizations involved and have harmful implications for the service users, staff and other stakeholders who have supported and been involved in the project. A high-profile example of this has been the Integrated Children's System (ICS) (Ince and Griffiths 2010). The ICS was planned to be an integrated IT system to collect information about children in need to facilitate the processes of assessment, planning and intervention to support multi-agency working. Whilst the initial ICS plan has not been completely abandoned, its current development is considerably different from what was initially envisaged. These failures occur across all sectors of the economy, and the high-level example of the NHS information system is well documented. The size of the organization has no discernible effect on whether the organization is going to be more or less successful in achieving these changes.

This chapter will start by helping you to make links between your project and your organization's strategy and the role that business planning plays in relation to project development and management. We will be looking at how you might go about designing a project and you will be introduced to a process of 'scoring' to help you select a project. We will be touching on the importance of resources and risk when managing a project and the importance of stakeholder involvement. Finally, we shall articulate the benefits of proposed projects in seeking to deliver service improvements.

The link between organizational strategy and projects

It is important to ensure that the organizational strategy is aligned to the goals of the project. This helps to ensure that the plans to 'get things done' are linked directly to *how* things might be done, so that priority is given by all parts of the organization to the project delivery. The use of robust project methodology with its structured approaches, together with critical use of tools and techniques, is important to increase the chances of success.

The business planning process

Hafford-Letchfield (2010) identifies a number of key steps in the business planning process, summarized as follows.

Understanding the organization's mission

Whilst language such as 'mission' might not be normal terminology in social work and social care, it is a term used in business to identify the reason why the organization exists, or in other words the purpose of the organization. Normally within the mission statement you might expect to see statements that highlight:

- what the organization is
- what the organization does
- why the organization undertakes what it does.

An example of this can be found in an organization's annual report. For example, the Annual Report for 2007 of the largest UK children's charity, Barnardo's, highlights:

Barnardo's vision is that the lives of all children and young people should be free from poverty, abuse and discrimination. Our purpose is to help the UK's most vulnerable children and young people transform their lives and fulfil their potential. (Barnardo's 2007, p.7)

The remainder of this section of the Barnardo's Annual Report then details the services it provides and how it is funded.

Organizational objectives

Organizational objectives are normally the long-term goals of the organization, that is, its 5–10-year plans. Once the organization has a clear mission it is customary for it also to set objectives. These objectives are normally measurable and set out what the organization will achieve within defined timescales. This type of statement could include:

- detailing the types of services the organization may provide and the turnover of these services (either in respect of numbers of people or perhaps even financially)

- the social and community work that the organization may undertake

- its environmental impact.

These objectives are often aligned to the organization's strategy. Continuing with the example of Barnardo's, some of the objectives listed in its annual report include: 'Deliver growth in fee and grant income for service provision of at least six per cent' (2010, p.7). This is then reflected in its plans for 2010–13 (Barnardo's 2010, p.11) which includes: 'Grow our direct work with children, as measured by our spend on children's services, by 15 per cent over the three years of the Business Plan.' As a result we can begin to see the linkages between the strategic objectives of the organization and its operational planning and service delivery.

Intermediate goals

These highlight how the organization plans to achieve its objectives. This would also take into consideration its strategic plans, annual budgets, planned projects and its current level of operations, as we can see from the illustration provided above.

In looking at each of the stages, consider the organization's tactical short-term goals as well as the individual plans for projects and operations. The strategic plans found at this level of planning set out how the organization aims to achieve the objectives that are identified in the stage above. These strategies and the resources that are being allocated to them identify the key organizational priorities. These may include:

- Budget allocations (possibly even covering several years).

- Business unit or service milestones against objectives. This may include miniaturized plans under each objective showing the key milestones to achievement.

- Programmes, operations and projects that are or will be undertaken within the organization. These are normally developed through a process of negotiation but clearly identify the key priorities that are being taken forward. Whilst it may not appear in this document, you would normally expect to find a set of further tactical plans on how each of these programmes, operations and projects will be achieved.

Project selection

It is important that projects are aligned to the strategic goals of the organization and service and these criteria are therefore key in the selection of projects, as most organizations do not have the resources to commit to all proposed initiatives identified. Examples of the types of criteria that might be used within organizations include:

- How well does the proposal link with other relevant organizational projects or strategies?

- What is the extent to which the project proposal meets the service's or organization's objectives and outcomes?

- How well does the project proposal meet stakeholder needs (in particular service users), provide benefits to its stakeholders and promote community involvement? Is there evidence of service user, staff and wider support for the project?

- Does the project identify the resources to deliver and is the project achievable?

- Is the project innovative and can it deliver the required change?

- Is the project economically, socially and environmentally sustainable?

- Does the project offer value for money?

- Are there demonstrable commitments to achieving equalities?

Some organizations which frequently consider the selection of projects, or who need to score project bids submitted to them, may often use a structured scoring mechanism to undertake this.

Project selection scoring

In any tender or consideration of a project, there is normally a transparent process of evaluation and this is often achieved using a systematic scoring method. This is particularly important as most organizations need to demonstrate for accountability or legal reasons that the process has been fair, transparent and robust. To illustrate the use of this possible system, we will make use of Deborah's case example from Chapter 2. The authors are not aware of any scoring system that was used by Deborah's employer and so the system discussed below has been developed for our purpose here to illustrate how this type of system might be used. In Deborah's case the organization was requiring reductions in budgetary expenditure of all services. Managers were required to put forward business plans to demonstrate how they would achieve this saving, while still meeting regulatory and legal and safeguarding requirements. Naturally, some professionals may argue that this is not possible and seek to not engage in this process, but this argument is beyond the remit of this book.

Within this example the organization needs to review each of the proposals, and would normally decide on a maximum numerical score that a project could attain and devise a metric to be used to gain this score. For instance it could be decided that the maximum score that a project could attain is, say, 100 points and that a project must achieve at least 65 points to pass the threshold for further detailed consideration. Those projects which do not meet the 65-point threshold would not be eligible for funding or in a tender process would no longer be considered. It should, however, be recognized that this type of evaluation system does not mean that all projects that meet the threshold would be funded; rather, the number of bids being considered is reduced for later consideration. Below, we consider a project scoring system example to illustrate the argument.

As we identified above in the selection criteria, checklist questions would be given a score (e.g. this could be a score between 0 and 5, which can be converted to a percentage to achieve the 100 points we highlighted earlier). To simplify the process and to ensure transparency, each score would be rounded up to the nearest whole number.

In this example, each criterion is assessed against a number of checklist questions (see Table 3.1) and the average score (between 0 and 5) is then converted into a percentage mark contributing to the overall total of 100.

In addition to these scores, each criterion is also given a weighting, which identifies the importance given to each of the criteria within the organization or for the tender invitation. An example of a possible weighting system is summarized below:

1. *Programme Criteria (45%)*

   Delivers legal, regulatory and organizational/service objectives (10%)

   Integrates with stakeholder priorities and programmes (10%)

   Project management and delivery (10%)

   Achieves savings required (5%)

   Integrates organizational priorities (5%)

   Availability of support and resources (5%)

2. *Wider Criteria (15%)*

   Project is sustainable over three-year budgetary period (10%)

   Achieves equal opportunity commitments (5%)

3. *Other Criteria (40%)*

   Meets the specified service requirements (25%)

   Stakeholder needs identified and incorporated (5%)

   Partnership arrangements are agreed and achievable (5%)

   Supports improved service outcomes (5%)

By weighting each of the criteria categories (e.g. Programme Criteria), you can see the importance being placed on each of the criteria and the sub-criteria in turn. These criteria and their marking should be made available to those putting forward projects or tender bids. Each of these criteria will be marked on a scale of 0–5 such as:

5   Ideal, or close to ideal, detailed evidence of quality and delivery

4   Detailed evidence of delivery and quality provided

3   Detailed evidence provided

1   General supporting statements provided

0   Not robust; supporting statements irrelevant or poor

As the proposal or tender will be reviewed by a number of people independently of each other, the rationale for each of these scores (0–5) will need to be specific, clear and detailed to ensure consistency in the judgements used in this selection process. These would normally be fully documented (see Table 3.1). It would be good practice for this scoring system to be piloted by people not involved in the selection system beforehand to ensure that any difficulties are identified and resolved before it is used in the final evaluation. This transparency and detail is required to account for decisions and to demonstrate due process if challenged, for example under European Union Competition Law.

Table 3.1 Project scoring criteria

Programme Criteria (45%)	Score (0–5) (completed by reviewer)	Evidence (links to tender specification or organizational business plan)
Delivers organizational/service objectives (10%)		Scores of 0 will not be considered for funding
How well does the project meet the organization/service objectives?		
Does the project ensure improved outcomes for the organization and service users?		
Will the project improve quality and reduce errors?		

Now having looked at how you might use criteria, the 'On the Spot' activity in Box 3.1 gives you an opportunity to apply this to your own practice area.

Operationalizing definitions is important as it helps to ensure that everyone involved in grading the proposal is doing so using similar criteria. These criteria should be clear and link directly to the requirements specified in the Project Initiation Document discussed in Chapter 1. This clarity enables external scrutiny such as audits or in legal disputes or contests. In comparing your responses with those of a colleague, you are likely to identify that these criteria need to be developed, piloted, evaluated and revised through several iterations before they would be ready for use.

Box 3.1

'On the Spot' – Identifying project proposal criteria

Using either a project you have been involved in or one of the service user perspectives from Chapter 2, identify four criteria that you would use to evaluate the stakeholder measure of a project proposal and ensure that their requirements are met.

1. How would you operationalize/define this?

2. Would these criteria stand up to external scrutiny and why?

3. Consult with a colleague and ask them for their views. Identify any differences from your own.

Risks and opportunities of project funding

In reviewing possible funding available for projects there are two key points of view to consider, namely that of the project owner and that of the contractor. Project funding may occur as a result of ring-fenced budgets or particular seed funding being made available by the government to promote policy objectives such as the Telecare Capital Grant and Telecare Revenue Grant (SSIA 2011). This grant is important as it aims to equip 10,000 homes in Wales with Telecare equipment and sensors, to support vulnerable people to stay within their homes rather than to move into residential care.

Whilst not all project managers may be directly responsible for budgets, budgeting remains important particularly if shortage of funds and resources places the delivery of the project in jeopardy. Available funds or resources (such as people) are an important aspect of the successful implementation of projects. These may be allocated directly for a project, result from restructuring of services, be resources reallocated from other priorities, or even result from policy reform.

Managing costs is a key role for project managers, and success of this task increases the likelihood that the project is both viable and a worthwhile undertaking. Financial risk is a key area of risk in any project. In any large project it is normal that financial support would be available for the project manager in order to enable them to undertake this task. Using Table 3.2 as an example of a simple budget statement, we can see that estimating costs is a key measure in seeking to control the financial aspects of a project. This example budget may therefore typify the budget and expenditure of introducing new equipment to support mobility within a residential care facility, in which new building and equipment installation, the retraining of staff and cover for these staff are required whilst they undertake this. As a result the budget statement would normally involve four aspects, namely:

1. Estimating the future expenditure of the project (normally the project budget).

2. Monitoring actual financial expenditure.

3. Identifying the variance – the difference between these two figures (b − a).

4. Action that needs to be taken as a result of the variance.

In thinking about the costs that are normally incurred in a project, these are usually as a result of:

- *Human resources.* This includes the cost of all people involved either directly or indirectly in the project. Within this form of calculation the cost can be worked out either as the total cost involved or in the hours worked. The latter would naturally require the organization to be clear about the cost per hour for each of the hours worked to calculate the monetary value. All projects have a human resource cost, whether it is salaries of existing staff or additional budget requirements for the employment of temporary staff.

- *Equipment.* This is the cost of equipment used in delivering the project. Equipment does not include consumables, but rather equipment that is used in the project but that may also be used in other future projects. This might include IT equipment which is used in organizational change programmes and is therefore reused in multiple presentations and projects.

- *Materials.* These are normally the consumables that are used in the delivery of a project, but might also include stationery, printing, etc.

- *Subcontracting.* This includes material and labour costs of subcontracting tasks to outside contractors.

- *Management and administration.* These are the costs for the management of the project and include project managers and administration as well as costs for the project office and specialized software to manage the project.

- *Inflation.* When inflation is low this is an issue that sometimes can be overlooked, but in days of higher inflation and longer-term projects it may be a significant risk, particularly if the project is a fixed-price project (no cost increases can be accommodated).

- *Contingencies.* This can be termed the reserve budget and usually allows the project manager a limited amount of financial tolerance. For example, in a large-scale project, budget reserves may be held to meet higher costs of procurement due to inflation than had previously been budgeted for.

Table 3.2 Budget and expenditure – for period 6

Item	Budget (a)	Actual spend (b)	Variance (b − a)	Reason	Action taken
Human resources	£45,000	£47,500	£2,500	Illness, agency cover	
Equipment	£63,000	£60,000	−£3,000	Not all equipment delivered	
Materials	£27,000	£45,000	£18,000	Cost increases	
Subcontracting	£5,700	£1,200	−£4,500	Not required	
Management and admin	£6,000	£6,000	£0		
Contingencies	£28,000	£28,000	£0		
Total	£174,700	£187,700	£13,000		Contingency funding may be required if future cost over-run remains

Stakeholders in projects

For all projects the key stakeholders, project success criteria and resources available for delivery are crucial. Whilst it is important to understand and engage with stakeholders, recognition of the project customer is also important. Conventionally there are two main groups of 'customer':

- *External customers* – where an organization or supplier undertakes to deliver a project for another organization and is paid for this project delivery. Examples of this type of project may be the delivery of a new IT system or the commissioning of a new care facility or hospital.

- *Internal customers* – where a project is undertaken within the organization and may for instance include projects where the organization is undertaking a project to meet its own business requirements. Examples of this type of project may include the redeployment of staff from one organization to another, the implementation of new staff remuneration (e.g. terms and conditions), reconfiguration of services or buildings, etc. In Chapter 2, Fiona's and Deborah's projects would both fall into this category.

As explored earlier, the idea or specification for a project can come from within the organization or from external customers. This, in part, may depend on the nature of the organization you are working for. If the organization specializes in undertaking project management for external clients, it is inevitable that the majority of project-based work will be funded from outside the organization.

Preparing tenders can frequently be viewed as mini-projects and often use the same project management skills as developing a full project. Tenders are used as a structured process to specify a series of requirements, for example domiciliary care by an organization wishing to procure these. A number of service providers, it is hoped, would normally submit a bid for the delivery of these services, detailing their costs and how they would achieve the detailed requirements specified in the issued tender. Prospective bidders provide their best price and specifications so that the organization that issued the tender can evaluate the proposed solution and obtain the best price for its delivery. This is due to them requiring significant amounts of planning, scoping, budgeting and development of evaluation work, even before any tender is awarded. Given the costs of such tendering, it is important for organizations to consider the potential costs of undertaking tendering work. This type of tender screening is often undertaken at a senior level, due to the amount of resources which may be required to meet the tender's need for specific documentation, time deadlines and submission requirements. Earlier in the chapter we reviewed the systematic scoring methodology and how this applied to a project as an example of this form of screening.

The elements of written and verbal specifications, whether obtained through customer discussions, queries or agreed changes, all contribute to the scope of the project. These are normally clearly specified in a project contract and often will detail payments, deadlines, milestones, delivery conditions and details on invoicing. Failure to meet contractual deadlines can result in penalty payments (if specified in the contract) to the tender client, but also may result in a damaged reputation for the contractor or even consequential losses to the contractor from miscalculated costs or timing. An example of this can be seen in the high-profile failure of the National Offender Management Information System (NAO 2009), which was designed as a single offender management system across the probation and prison service, and the consequent escalation in costs and damage to reputations.

Organizational challenges

It is important in social work and social care organizations that are undertaking projects that the right people, resources, communication and skills are available and utilized to meet the agreed project objectives. Whilst organizations may have different structures, it is clear that there needs to be clarity in respect of accountability and what each member of the project team will be contributing to the project. Communication within project teams is vital to ensure that the team members are well motivated and clear about their roles and tasks. In contrast, poor communication often results in uncertainty about responsibility, accountability ambiguity, poor motivation and missed deadlines, resulting in cost and resource overruns together with difficult team working.

Organizational structure

Structures in organizational projects can be functional, in which the management of the organization delegates responsibility to different units to complete their respective aspects of the overall project. An example of this might be in the development of a new service, such as a social care provider establishing a new home visiting service for vulnerable people who are isolated and need additional social support. In that instance responsibility for recruitment of staff is undertaken by the Human Resource Department, the development of buildings becomes the responsibility of the Estates Department, IT is responsible for technology, etc. In organizations where the structure is functionally determined the project manager's power can be very weak and she or he can feel disempowered and as a result may be better referred to as a 'project coordinator'.

A further structure is the use of project teams, in which a project team is responsible for the delivery of the project and has its own structure and resources, including staff and administration. These staff may be recruited from within or outside the organization, with a dedicated project manager to lead the process. The advantage of this type of structure is that it is relatively simple, the skilled resources are dedicated to the task and not faced with conflicts over commitments, and it can result in a high degree of team cohesiveness and commitment due to the shared goal (Gray and Larson 2005). A clear disadvantage is that it may be expensive and, for smaller-scale projects, this level of resourcing may be impractical.

An alternative style of project management, which is more of a hybrid between the two previous approaches, is that of matrix organizational management. In this structure, similarly skilled people are joined to enable the sharing of skills and expertise across boundaries. The staff as a result report to two different managers, both the project manager and their functional manager. The advantage of this arrangement is that it uses resources more effectively and is flexible. There are also disadvantages, such as that it can be stressful, result in conflict and tension, and requires excellent management and leadership to be successful (Gray and Larson 2005).

The use of integrated project management teams enables their project managers to have significant power and influence in order to deliver the project; this might mean having influence considerably above departmental managers. An example of an integrated project management team may be the inclusion of project-specific experts from health, social work/social care, construction, finance, etc. in a dedicated project management team, where their sole responsibility is the delivery of the project, such as the design and delivery of a new mental health crisis centre. This clarity of role, responsibility and relationship may be an indicator of experience in project delivery.

It is important to remember that all projects are temporary; by this we mean that they have a start and end date and the project team that supports the project delivery may cease to exist after the end date. Clarity about role and handover enables the end of the project to be efficient, but equally important is the recognition of those involved in these changes.

Culture

The most difficult aspect of the project is ensuring an appropriate organizational culture. Its importance is underlined by the impact that culture has on how a project is undertaken and the way in which project management is implemented. For example, considering your own organization, if it is risk adverse, how would it react to a high-risk project – would it be stopped? Another way of understanding culture would be to ask whether all members of the project team receive the same recognition (perhaps a bonus or honorarium) for successful completion as everyone else in their team – if this is offered at all. Are staff members who have worked on the team reallocated to a new problem, found other jobs or made redundant?

Systems and process

Resource management often poses a significant problem for many organizations. Whilst some central systems such as accounting may be able to use the same core financial systems with revised reporting arrangements, other systems may need to be developed. These may include new systems to deal with risk management, action tracking and benchmarking. It is often these parts of the infrastructure that support information management and so facilitate decision-making.

The 'On the Spot' activity in Box 3.2 is an opportunity for you to bring together these organizational challenges for a project of your own.

Box 3.2

'On the Spot' – Organizational opportunities and challenges

Using a project you have been involved in (or you may wish to reflect on one of the projects considered in Chapter 2), consider the importance of culture, structure, systems and process in your own organization.

1. What challenges can you identify?

2. What opportunities might there be?

3. Develop a brief number of action points of how you might maximize the opportunities and minimize the challenges.

Key reflection points

The culture, structure and processes of an organization are key to managing to successfully control and deliver projects. Often we are able to see this most clearly as newcomers within an organization. The longer you spend in an organization, the more you begin to accept its norms. As a project manager with responsibility to deliver your project, it is important that you are able to critically analyse these aspects, review the links to the project and develop plans to mitigate or address the challenges you and your team will experience. These issues would normally be discussed directly with the project sponsor and agreement sought about how this is best managed.

Projects and planning

Projects are often open to the risks of uncertain events, and normally considerable effort is invested in trying to predict and manage these. When significant risk events occur, they can have an enormous impact on the project in terms of outcomes, costs and process. Project management literature seeks to manage this by attempting to manage the human factors that are often seen as the cause of these events (Gray and Larson 2005; Pender 2001). As a result there is a heavy reliance on project documentation, process and protocols in project management systems. However, despite this, unexpected events can still occur, partly as some events are difficult to predict or identify and they will impact on the project despite efforts to manage them. As yet there remain few publications in the project management literature on how people respond to unexpected events.

Geraldi, Lee-Kelley and Kutsch (2010) identified that projects are inherently uncertain and often are impacted by unexpected events. Attempts to manage these unexpected events or changes are undertaken through risk management mechanisms in order to introduce elements of control and management and are discussed in more detail in Chapter 7. The purpose therefore of risk management in this context is to assess and manage future risks so that they may be resolved before they impact adversely on the project outcome (Chapman and Ward 2002; Hafford-Letchfield 2010). These unexpected risks can range from bankruptcy of the client, to external environmental crisis, to changes to the scope of the project. Geraldi *et al.* (2010) identified three mechanisms to support successful reactions to unexpected events, namely:

- A responsive functioning structure at organizational level, in which key staff have full senior management support and a significant degree of freedom to make and implement decisions.

- Good interpersonal relationships at a group level, which facilitate engagement with stakeholders, enabling solutions to be negotiated with effective communication.

- Competent individuals with effective leadership and team management skills who are able to manage stressful circumstances and who have a high degree of self-awareness.

Planning the project is something almost everyone would agree is a necessity, and in undertaking this it is necessary to ensure that you address the following principles:

- Clarify purpose – the purpose of project planning is to ensure that a project plan is developed that facilitates the executing and control of the project.

- Ongoing planning – given the complexity of project planning, it is unlikely that any plan is developed just once. As the plan is developed and consulted on, it is likely that iterations will need to be undertaken and further planning undertaken. This has been our experience in writing this book!

- Project planning requires considerable documentation to specify the full extent of the plan, resources, timescales, etc. and contain all the information necessary to successfully control a project. It should contain all the information necessary to ensure that if there was a change in project manager then the new person would be able to step into the role.

- Clarity around stakeholder expectations – these should be clear before the start of any project and include details of responsibilities, quality, risk management, project management and any procurement.

- Project planning is undertaken from the bottom up, as it must ensure that it has included adequate time for consultation, facilitation, questioning and feedback.

Project life cycles

Most projects have a clear start and end point, with a variety of 'milestones' of progress that can easily be identified. Within the project life there are a number of key stakeholders and roles as follows:

- *The client.* This is the person or commissioner who has procured the project or who is selling it to a third party.

- *The contractor.* This is the organization that is responsible to the client for the completion of the project.

- *The project manager.* This is the person normally employed by the contractor (e.g. the social work and social care organization) to plan and manage the project. It is normally this person's responsibility to ensure it is completed on time, to budget and to project specification.

Phases in projects

There are a number of phases (steps) within a project life cycle, some of which can overlap – for example, some procurement can start before the final design is complete in order to meet exacting timescales. Typically a project may involve a number of phases from the time that it is initially considered until it is finally completed. This will be explored in more detail in Chapter 5.

Benefits map

As projects become more complicated and are integrated more clearly within the business processes of organizations, the performance of the service or process may require more than just the 'successful' completion of the project. For instance, opening a new community service to try to reduce older people's emergency admissions to hospital in which they are offered intensive and high levels of nursing care within their own homes. It is likely that the new service will have a significant potential impact on a range of services for older people; not only in reducing unnecessary hospital admissions but also requiring protocols and systems to ensure that primary care and social work teams fully understood what support could be safely provided in the community, what would trigger hospital admissions and the linkages with existing community support services (e.g. for falls prevention). Thus, considerable work is needed to review and redevelop the whole system of care and support provided, to ensure that its implementation is appropriate and effective. The following stages are therefore important:

- Allow time and space for members of the unit and community teams to develop new skills, renegotiate service boundaries and protocols, and negotiate changes to the patterns of working and referrals.

- Encourage the new service processes to develop. This might include facilitating stakeholders to gain more experience of the use of the changed service, obtain feedback on these changes and make changes to the service to meet identified needs.

- Encourage wider understanding amongst all stakeholders of the new service and its links to other community, residential and hospital services.

- Continually evaluate the experience of stakeholders using the service and so improve its effectiveness and efficiency.

You can therefore see that this new service must be seen within the context and range of the overall provision of older people's services in that area. As a result, the planning stages of the project should have analysed, understood and shared the agreed service objectives and performance to:

- influence the design and operation of the new service

- ensure all stakeholders understand how to access the new service and allow time for benefits of the change to be realized. It goes without saying, but the views of all stakeholders would be important in evaluating this.

The benefits map undertaken at the start of the project should therefore identify all the potential benefits, but also highlight areas where further analysis is required so that these can be incorporated into the overall project design, such as the reduction in hospital admissions in the example given.

Chapter summary

This chapter has explored the context of project management, recognizing the importance of business planning to the development of projects. Failure to ensure strategic alignment between the goals and objectives of the organization and any proposed project is likely to result in little support being gained for its implementation. Any such proposal must therefore meet the requirements specified and be able to robustly demonstrate the achievements of these requirements. Recognition of the importance of project selection tools in the evaluation of proposals helps to strengthen discipline in the development and implementation of projects. Stakeholder involvement in the development, implementation and evaluation of projects is critical, and structures, systems and processes established to manage projects should facilitate this engagement as well as the delivery of the project.

Action checklist

- Ensure that you closely align your project to the organization's strategic objectives.

- Make sure that the project has agreed goals that all stakeholders have signed up to.

- Clarify and make certain that the project benefits are clear and achievable.

Chapter 4

Project Management
for Service Users

Introduction

In recent years there have been widespread attempts to involve service users together with other stakeholders such as partner agencies in the design, delivery and evaluation of social work and social care services (SCIE 2004). Repeated guidance and reports highlight the importance and recognition of stakeholder and, more particularly, service user involvement, but also the difficulty in recognizing financially their contributions of time (Turner and Beresford 2005). This would include service users being faced by challenges such as benefits, accusations of fraud and concerns about people being available for work (Turner and Beresford 2005).

This chapter aims to reflect on stakeholders' experience of projects undertaken within social work and social care and utilizes the narrative of two service users (Rashida and Colin) who have been actively engaged in projects, as well as the perspective of an NHS stakeholder (Claire). In hearing their stories, we plan to reflect on their thoughts and ideas in light of the ideas explored in the book. Whilst there is no one stakeholder view, the importance of the themes and perspectives they provide us with is a useful and suitable staging post to reflect on how we undertake projects and the impact it has on those who we engage and design services for. In order to decide on who to involve it is important for us to consider the wide range of potential stakeholders, including those hard-to-reach communities, for example children and people with complex drug and alcohol problems. As a result, we may need to engage differently with certain stakeholder groups despite them perhaps living in very similar areas.

The promotion of democratic approaches to citizenship and civil rights helps to support the shift of power, control and accountability (SCIE 2006). Participation can manifest in three interrelated forms (Webb 2006):

- *Action.* This includes listening, sharing of information and responding to questions.

- *Processes.* This involves engagement in decision-making and agenda-setting.

- *Values.* This includes ideas of democracy and inclusion.

Many of these forms of engagement can be identified through the service user narratives below. By including these contributions, we hope that you hear both the voices of those who have contributed but also many of those who contribute, but do not have a direct voice in this book. All contributions have been anonymized in respect of the agencies and others involved.

Colin's experience

After being an inpatient I was referred to a Day Hospital, where I was allowed to become involved with learning difficulties patients, helping them with reading and writing, by making flash cards on the computer. I did produce a monthly newsletter, the '*T*' *Times*, for a few years till a new nurse started to criticize both the content and layout. When I handed it over to her as I was no longer accessing that service she did nothing, and my last issue was not published.

I was also involved in a training and employment project where service users were encouraged to get involved. To start with this was a bit detrimental to my mental health as my IT skills meant all the computer problems were referred to me or the trainer. Eventually we understood each other's limitations and when the trainer and administrator left I took on the role of admin/trainer/network supervisor. I encouraged the manager to use IT and we did a lot of designing and printing for the Centre which meant we could buy more computers and help more people. We even started a service user project which is still functioning in only a slightly different guise, three outreach centres which sadly were only funded for a few years, and a service user organization which works with the commissioners to maintain mental health services in Coventry and Warwickshire. Of course I still was a client, so when we received a referral from the Day Hospital if there was any information missing I had to get it from them. This was easy with the clerk at the Centre but I had to be careful of the manager as confidentiality meant I could not access another patient's records. That manager had difficulty communicating with we service users. She seemed to patronize us till she had her own problems and became a good Community Psychiatric Nurse.

A further experience was in a joint NHS/Social Care day centre, where the manager did try to encourage service users to be involved, but she had a typical civil service way of doing things. She wondered why nobody would attend her user meetings which were strictly controlled – if you wanted to bring up something it had to be on the agenda beforehand or wait for Any Other Business. This is no good for people without a short-term memory or on sedating drugs who forget what they need to say. I did manage to work with her (or in spite of her) and was involved in introducing subjects and teaching at the Centre. But unlike my previous experience it was difficult to get any payment for work done.

As a married man with a wife, children, house, car, etc., I needed to earn more than just the benefits, therefore was always looking for more things to do as a way to get me back into work. I heard of a training course on Wellness Recovery Action Planning (WRAP) so I became a trainer and also became involved in the training of social workers, medical students, clinical psychology students and now students on nursing degree courses.

I have been a member of a couple of GP patient panels and at one time was involved in doing Quality Audits on GPs before the cutbacks some years ago. This meant I was recruited by some researchers who were looking at the effectiveness of PPI in health. This was a far cry from the treatment I got from the panel which was set up to oversee the plans, consultation and implementation of the building of a new Medium Secure Unit where I was the token service user. Now I even have my photo in the report for one project and my views are respected. I even managed to get employment as an Associate Mental Health Act Manager much to the disgust of certain professionals who think service users should not have that sort of power. My Associate Mental Health Act Manager's job means I am one of three hospital managers who sit on hearings of people who are sectioned, often chairing the panel. The demise of my mental health was partly brought on by back problems developed working in industry.

My experiences of transition consisted of attending services that were for adults (who were then classified as 18–65 years of age). So when I was approaching my 65th birthday I asked at my Care Plan review what service there was for older people. Although the answer was 'I don't know but I'll find out', they never did. The health and social care establishment terminated my service at 65. Because I was doing voluntary work there, the charity let me continue, but over the years before and since, legislation became so strict that the amount of work I could do was reduced. Years previously I had supervised clients single-handed at weekends, maintained the computers, produced databases to store client records and automatically sent out letters. This work was taken from me due to health and safety rules and nationalization of IT and other functions. Due to social security rules I also found that my benefits would cease and my old age pension was considerably less money. I was not paying tax on my benefits, which made matters worse. By that time my marriage had broken down and I had to move into rented accommodation. My rent was going up but my small company pension was not. I needed paid work as well as the voluntary jobs, hence getting involved with anything that paid more than travel. I have got involved with the church which has a stall where I can get good quality second-hand or new things for very little, so at present can make ends just about meet as long as I stay healthy.

As I mentioned earlier, the one project had some satellite projects. One was a shop and workshop which was initially funded by printing work we did for other centres. This ceased when the management was changed and that work dried up. For a short time we managed to get some funding as a publicity campaign from a big store chain but then the project charity started to close all the projects that were losing money. Although we were selling goods made by ourselves and social enterprises we lost the shop. Another project I was involved in was National Regeneration, funded for three years in deprived areas of the city, but because of all the legal requirements and the refurbishing of premises it took almost half that time to set them up, train the staff and get fully functioning. So we had just become somewhere that the locals would trust to solve their problems when we had to close our doors.

The self-help groups and user involvement organizations have various problems. People move on or there is not enough publicity to sustain them. The nature of long-term mental health problems is such that people cannot organize things long-term. Without funding to employ a manager the system can collapse. We have had to employ a manager in both services to keep things on track, and to attract funding now you have to be a charity and a company limited by guarantee. You have to find cheap financial and IT people and know all the latest ways of attracting money and complying with legislation.

When they were developing the Community Mental Health teams I was on the planning committee to develop a system that was universal, workable and acceptable to both staff and service users and carers. I have recently been involved in trying to smooth the transition from hospital back into the community by improving the housing and employment agencies' understanding of mental health problems. I have for years been involved in reviewing leaflets, procedures, letters and policies to make them easier to understand by all.

I am now approaching 70 years of age and am a radically different person from the one who managed Industrial Radiography laboratories in industry. I now know a lot about the long-term conditions I suffer from in the way that some of the people who have never experienced them just don't understand.

Rashida's experience

My name is Rashida. I was born in the UK. I am married and I have four children – three girls and one boy. I have been a carer for 21 years looking after my elderly mother-in-law who is aged 81 and suffers from rheumatoid arthritis and has a heart condition and also is now suffering from breast cancer. I am also a health care assistant working in a job with the NHS which I have been doing for nearly three years. I work with older people with dementia and mental health issues. I have been a service user consultant for seven years and throughout that I have had an opportunity to talk to social work students at university about my experiences as a carer, at the recall days that they do.

Furthermore, I have attended different workshops and stakeholder meetings and worked with project managers. Also I have taken part in interview panels for students, which has been the most wonderful and intriguing experience I have had. It has boosted my self-confidence and self-esteem, and this has enabled me to stand and deliver my voice and experience to the students; especially knowing that they will learn from listening to a true story of the everyday life of a carer. The most incredible part of lecturing the students is that they actually listen with interest and ask questions at the end of each session, which then gives me the opportunity to explain in more depth, and that makes me feel that they have understood the whole aspect of knowing the good and bad side of a carer and service user's life.

Payment issues

Payment issues can sometimes be difficult as you get some carer service users who claim benefits and they are only allowed minimum payment, but now that has been dealt with and the payment can be spread over the months. Also if you are working you have to pay taxes on any contribution you receive, which would be your own responsibility.

Empowering

Empowering service users to maximize their experience and prospects is a very valuable activity for students to hear and learn from. Also it is good for service users to get the opportunity to contribute as it helps them to open up and feel they are achieving something by telling their story. Students listen with enjoyment and take better interest with this activity or any involvement from service users or carers.

We have had chance to take part in podcast interviews, where we had social staff recording us being interviewed and questioned. It was a fantastic experience and this recording was to be put on the internet for the university to approach at any time or place.

Relationship with project managers

The relationship with project managers is very interesting and informative, and they are always there to assist us in any activity we are taking part in.

The managers are always willing to work round the carers and what will suit them best. Also we are given recognition for our activity and we also receive payments.

For the students, the quality of any kind of involvement and work with the service users and carers is crucial. It will have an excellent impact on them and will give them a wake-up call to what they may face when they go out into the working world as qualified social workers, and what possibilities they have to look out for in their placements. Service users and carers have worked really hard, and with all the cutbacks it will be a shame to see their involvement of work reduced within the university. Also it would have been great to see the work we do receive credits so that it can improve our future career prospects.

Claire's experience

Change is a way of life in the NHS and social care. As Director of Commissioning and Service Improvement in a small Primary Care Team (PCT) covering a population of 167,000, it was becoming clearer that the spectre of dementia in our population was becoming ever more real. Currently nationally, 570,000 people live with dementia, which describes a range of progressive, terminal brain diseases where age is the main risk factor and people need a range of complex health and social care services (DoH 2009a). Given the knowledge of the proposed policy, in 2008 the PCT commissioned a detailed analysis of dementia services ('a deep dive') to feed into our Joint Strategic Needs Assessment (JSNA), which is a joint health and social care analysis of health and social care needs in our community.

In addition to undertaking the 'deep dive', we commissioned the Alzheimer's Society and Senior Citizens' Forum to interview 100 people with dementia, or their family carer, to comment on their experiences of local services. These people were attracted through newspaper adverts, posters, leaflets and presentations to relevant interest groups. The resulting report, 'Now you see me, Now...' highlighted service gaps, suggested quality improvements, and described how people's lives had been affected by either the positive or negative experiences they had encountered when accessing local services. Numerous examples given by service users and carers referred to the whole pathway of their care, enabling them to share their experiences of interactions (or relationships) between PCT, local authority and voluntary and community groups. The report therefore, though commissioned by the PCT, was able to capture the bigger picture and was, at times, both complimentary and critical of a mixture of service areas and professions, which made dementia a concern for everybody.

This report of personal experiences, together with prevalence data and the strategic priorities of national policy, increased the profile of dementia within the local health economy and created the foundations for all agencies to find solutions together to some of the shortcomings in local provision. This was strengthened at a senior and corporate level across the whole health economy, with sign-up from both the Chief Executive of the PCT and Director of Adult and Community Well-being.

As the Director responsible for joint commissioning, I used the close working relationship with social care colleagues to make the case for change. Fortuitously, it was clear to all, backed by the evidence of the JSNA and the 'Now you see me, Now...' report, that dementia was truly a social and health care issue. However, the main factor in convincing all that immediate action was necessary was that research being undertaken and reported in order to prepare for the impending Department of Health policy and the warnings in the Wanless Report (DoH 2004) showed that health and social care communities had to take action to change the way that they were delivering care or we would not be able to afford care in the future.

Locally we undertook a public engagement process with a subsequent report produced. Regionally, we also participated in the West Midlands Pathway Development Group, learning and gathering data from other colleagues in the West Midlands. As a result of this work both locally and regionally, the West Midlands encouraged all health economies to designate dementia as one of their World Class Commissioning (DoH 2007b) priorities.

The National Dementia Strategy was launched in 2009 and encouraged the development of a local Dementia Strategy. The personalization agenda in social care also encouraged economies to address the needs of those with dementia and it was clear that there were sufficient levers in the local health and social care economy to undertake strategic and service changes. However, it was recognized by all stakeholders that such change would not happen overnight.

To reinforce the priority of 'change' a Strategic Commissioning Group was formed called 'Thinking Ahead', to make key decisions and, more importantly, to make change happen. This group included representatives from Social Care, Health, Joint Commissioning, service providers, the voluntary sector and people with direct experience of dementia. Each representative from a sector or profession came to the table not only with a sense of responsibility but also with a level of understanding and decision-making capabilities, and could drive through change quickly. This group used a Service Gap tool to rate service provision against the recommendations to create a review of current service provision. Using the information collated in the JSNA, the 'deep dive', the 'Now you see me, Now...' report and the policy recommendations, the 'Thinking Ahead' Group prioritized areas for improvement and spending allocation. Strategic prioritization meant that resources were protected for service developments, and the presence of the partnership ethos between the stakeholders noted above meant that greater efficiencies could be achieved in terms of addressing over- and under-capacity issues and a refocusing of resources to meet the strategic goals of the PCT outlined as part of their World Class Commissioning Strategic Plan.

It was clear that even an explicit message of intent about joint responsibility for improving experiences of people with dementia and their carers was not enough. It was important to demonstrate to service users and carers that the economy would actually take action to improve services and address the issues that were raised in the gap analysis, such as the need for the development of awareness training in health and social care to ensure that people with dementia stayed as healthy and enabled as possible. At every opportunity, partners were asked to work together on solutions and make progress.

In orchestrating a submission for National Demonstrator Site status for Dementia Peer Support (DoH 2009b), a Partnership Group was formed to create the model for service delivery with nearly 20 providers in attendance.

Although the national submission was unsuccessful, the pilot model was consulted upon through this Group which has absorbed the 'Thinking Ahead' Group and formed into a Commissioning Partnership Board to involve a broader mix of professionals, service users and carers, in the design and recommendation-making process. Commissioning Partnerships make recommendations to the Professional Executive Committee (PEC) and Board in order to inform prioritization and disinvestment decisions and bring together clinical expertise, patient experience and commissioning/ management facilitation and were designed to be a much more effective mechanism.

Investment in dementia services was prioritized in the operating plan of the PCT with the development of the first Admiral Nurse, a specialist nurse providing support for family carers. Also the Council, in their budgeting process, prioritized supporting respite and domiciliary care packages, and improved assessment for carers' needs, and together the Council and PCT prioritized addressing the training requirements of all professionals in the care of people with dementia. Our framework for joint commissioning included the social care policy 'Putting People First', and enabled leads in the local authority to facilitate the market development of future dementia services, whilst health colleagues worked with an external agency to develop a licensed, interactive demand and capacity tool to aid the planning of services for the future.

Lessons learnt have highlighted the need to collate information in new ways, in order to appropriately and adequately manage performance. Local and national measures are now included in all of our contracts and are monitored within a robust framework for performance within Joint Commissioning and Contracting. In addition, the Alzheimer's Society and Senior Citizens' Forum were commissioned again to interview service users to gauge experiences, whilst Public and Patient Engagement Leads within the PCT assisted with more mainstream, regular service user and carer feedback, in partnership with the Public Engagement Lead within the local authority.

At every opportunity, the health economy reinforced dementia as a local priority, which stretched across mental health, older people's services, social inclusion, social care and generalist and specialist services. This shared ownership and approach meant that people, both at strategic and operational levels, were prepared to provide joint solutions, or at least agree a joint approach. The Audit Commission (NAO 2010) released a report detailing the state of readiness of all PCTs to deliver the new dementia strategy and used the PCT as a case study of best practice. Dementia continues to be a priority for the health and social care economy.

As a project, conducted at a time when the NHS and social care was only just entering the 'age of austerity', this was seen to be a very effective model for joint commissioning and provision. An Audit Commission report for the Department of Health which was used to assess how ready health economies were for the implementation of the National Dementia Strategy used the project as a model of effective implementation. They reported that stakeholders worked well together developing new models of dementia care to meet the tsunami of need and commended the health economy for developing new services with service users and carers and also for using users and carers to evaluate all changes made. As explained, at the time of this project PCTs had experienced ten years of sustained growth in funding. Councils had received increased budgets year on year, and although their growth was not seen to be as generous as the NHS, there was still money in the system for innovation. Joint commissioning was working well after a period of uncertainty, following the Council accusing the PCT (whose previous director took a lead on managing the staff in joint commissioning) of not taking the Council's issues equally into account. Working together on this project was seen as real evidence that this relationship was now on track.

However, in the 2009/10 planning round, several things happened:

• It became clear that financial budgets in health and social care were going to be significantly reduced.

• The Adult Social Care Director left and was replaced by his deputy in a temporary acting role only.

• The Strategic Health Authority commissioned an investigation into spend across the region on continuing health care (CHC) and the PCT's spend was the second highest per patient in the region. The PCT was instructed to reduce its spend to the average across the region. This resulted in a review of all patients and of the CHC policy against the new CHC framework, and resulted in patients being taken off CHC funding as their conditions no longer qualified for CHC funding. Unfortunately, without CHC funding, the Council had to pick up some of the funding of patients, and given that their budgets were being significantly reduced already, this caused them significant concern.

- The Council lead party changed and the Chief Executive Officer (CEO) left. The finance director was promoted to CEO.

- PCTs were instructed to reduce their management costs (which included the Joint Commissioning Team) by 45 per cent.

Where the PCT had funded all of the extra dementia services in the first two years of the project because they had available budgets, since funding reduced dramatically it could no longer fund the planned improvements in years three and four alone. Unfortunately, because of the serious cuts in the Council's budgets and the added pressure of having to fund patients who were being removed from CHC funding, they could not offer any funding.

Dementia entered the PCT's prioritization process without the priority that had been assigned in previous years given the budget squeeze and did not even make the Council's process. This meant that no further investment was made in services by either the PCT or the Council. Relationships between the Council and the PCT became more tense due to the CHC issue.

Managing in a period of austerity creates challenges which, although linked to finances, are also about levels of trust, leadership, maturity, engagement and involvement. It also requires policy and incentives to be aligned in health and social care and a true health and social care community approach to solutions.

What we have seen from the latter stages of this case study are relationships falling apart as leaders retreat into their silo management, partly due to a need to protect their own finances (remember one of the main objectives of PCTs and Councils is to manage within their budget envelope) but also as a result of external drivers – an insistence of actions from the SHA to the PCT to implement spending reviews which would markedly affect working relationships, and also a drive from the Council Cabinet to save money at all costs by not replacing key leadership roles.

Public engagement in difficult decision-making takes time and investment, and with the cuts in management numbers in PCTs and Councils this is being lost. So what do we need in the future? We need a combination of new forms of public engagement and innovative policy-making. We need to build a consensus and understanding that there are no pain-free solutions for the future. We need to engage people in discussions about the consequences of all actions, get consensus, implement actions and stick to the policy. Mature joint working between social care and health care can create an environment where democratic accountability for involvement in decision-making can work. It needs mature and experienced leadership, joint risk management and a view that this is a total community issue. A Utopian idea perhaps – I hope not, for the sake of our children.

Chapter summary

Each of the service users' experiences demonstrates a wealth of understanding and perspectives and provides an insight into aspects of project delivery. As their experience varies, we can see the importance of their contributions to the success of projects and those themes such as partnership, clear focus on the project aims and the recognition and worth of each other's perspectives, knowledge and experience. We need therefore to ensure that we value all contributions (we take a wider perspective of this in Chapter 9). We cannot ensure whole systems change without this partnership and, as we have previously highlighted, the success of a project is dependent on more than a sum of its component parts.

The recognition of challenges for service users enables projects to support and facilitate service user engagement whilst ensuring their full and ongoing participation. This only happens when all stakeholders work jointly towards an agreed outcome, with clear, honest and transparent dialogue about our perspectives, experience and knowledge. This may mean that we have disagreements; we need to seek compromise or negotiate new shared understandings and solutions. These types of discussion are often easier in the early stages of the project when we are seeking to scope and plan the project and the culture of openness and honesty can be drawn on later when implementation decisions may become more complex and challenging.

Action checklist

- Review the purpose of the project and ensure that all stakeholders have been fully involved and their contributions actively sought.

- Develop a clear communication strategy and agree with all stakeholders how this will be implemented.

- Ensure that all engagement is undertaken honestly, transparently and according to appropriate ethical standards.

- Develop a critical and inclusive project environment to facilitate joint working.

Chapter 5

Managing Your Project

Introduction

In Chapter 3 we considered project management as a process for managing change. With that in mind we are going to move on to look at how this might apply to your own work and to explore the process of project management in more detail. We will be taking you through the skills required to plan the life cycle of a project, including managing the process from beginning to end.

What makes a project a project?

In Chapter 2 we presented three case studies which illustrate how diverse projects can be. At first glance they appear to have little in common, but there are specific attributes which are present in all projects.

A beginning and an end

As pointed out in Chapter 1, every project has a clearly visible beginning and end. This does not necessarily mean that it is a short-term enterprise; a project can last for years. For example, developing a new residential care facility may involve building new premises or at the very least will require identification of appropriate premises in addition to planning the service delivery. We also saw in Fiona's case study that a project can be a much more contained piece of work. So the length of time is immaterial – the identifying factor is that the end of the project is clear from the outset.

You might have wondered, in relation to Deborah's case study, which involved scoping the development of a community scheme, whether this is in fact a project. This is because, if it successfully identifies a way of using volunteers effectively, at the end, having achieved its intended outcomes, it will become a long-term service. It is important to be able to identify the point of changeover. At the point that the service is set up and becomes an integral part of the team's service delivery package, it ceases to be a project. Similarly, in our example of establishing a residential care facility, once the home has opened and is providing an ongoing service, it is no longer a project.

If you consider the history of many of the services currently being offered in social work and social care you will no doubt find that they began as projects; for example, the development of multi-professional youth offending teams in the UK in response to the 1998 Crime and Disorder Act (HMSO 1998) and more recently the roll-out of personalized budgets for service users since 2008 (DoH 2006). The scoping, the consultation, the planning and the development were all part of a project prior to the service becoming established, so project management is something that we have been doing in social work and social care for a long time. However, it is used increasingly as we try to respond to rapid change. There are tensions that need to be considered in relation to this approach as local authorities and large voluntary sector agencies can be slow to respond to change because of their hierarchical and bureaucratic structure which results in detailed procedures. Projects may be used as a means of responding to change more quickly, but they are still operating within the same organization, so embedding and sustaining change can be challenging.

Uniqueness

Second, every project is unique. This is one of the most challenging aspects of project management and we will look at the implications for leadership skills in the next chapter, because this means that project managers are always working in uncharted waters. How many times as an operational manager do you think, 'I've done this before...', 'this worked last time...' or 'I'll know how to do that better next time...'? One of our coping strategies in management is that we build up a body of 'on the job' tacit and experiential knowledge.

As we noted from the case studies, what stands out instantly is their differences rather than their similarities. It is their individuality that compels a shared methodology and approach to project management as a means of providing structure and some conformity which at least enables project managers to learn from the experience of other project managers. This is important because if we view each project as completely original we run the risk of floundering or of 'reinventing the wheel', so the project manager needs to be able to transfer learning from the success and failure of other projects. The skill is in determining what is transferable.

Project life cycle

The term 'project life cycle' is apt as a project is an organic entity and project management is not unlike parenting in some ways. You have to nurture your project, set clear boundaries and, although the nature of your input will change over time, even as it is reaching maturity it will still demand your time, attention and resources. Taking your eye off the ball can lead to unpredictable results and, although it will be challenging in ways you had not foreseen, when your project is ultimately successful you will experience a huge sense of satisfaction and pride.

However, in an attempt to provide a more business management approach to the subject, models of project management have emerged over the years which break the cycle down into stages. While this can seem a little mechanistic, it does provide a structure which ensures we have addressed the key tasks.

PRINCE2

One of the most widely used approaches to project management is PRINCE2, which was introduced in Chapter 1. This suggests seven stages of the life cycle, as shown in Table 5.1.

Table 5.1 The PRINCE2 project life cycle

Stage	Typical tasks
Starting up	Preparing the project brief, appointing the team
Initiating	Developing the business case, planning
Directing	Authorizing the project plan
Controlling a stage	Assessing and reviewing progress
Managing stage boundaries	Updating
Managing product delivery	Delivering the project
Closing	Evaluation

NHS model

This model has been adapted by the NHS Institute for Innovation and Improvement to relate more closely to the specific nature of health projects (Table 5.2).

Table 5.2 NHS project life cycle

Stage	Typical tasks
Start out	Establishing a rationale for improvement work and gaining support from a sponsor
Define and scope	Undertaking root cause analysis and establishing a project structure
Measure and understand	Assessing the gap between where we are now and where we want to be
Design and plan	Planning the activities needed to close the gap
Pilot and implement	Testing out proposed changes
Sustain and share	Ensuring implementation and dissemination

Source: based on NHS (2011)

The differences between the two models are subtle but significant and relate, to some degree, to the difference between a product development model (PRINCE2) and a service development model (NHS). The importance of scientific measurement and testing as part of a risk management strategy and an emphasis on evidence-based practice are more clearly visible in the NHS model. Both models are useful as a reference point in social work project management, but we also need to be clear about the subtleties of the differences which are specific to social work.

Project Management Institute

The Project Management Institute (PMI) suggests a very straightforward five-stage cycle which is similar to PRINCE2 in that its design makes clear the tasks which need to be completed at each stage. However, the five stages can be aligned with Tuckman's (1965) five stages of group development – forming; storming; norming; performing; and adjourning – which describe the process of how a group works together. Tuckman suggests that at its inception a group is quite tentative and members need to become familiar with each other so that they will be able to challenge each other in order to develop accepted ways of working which enable them to carry out their role effectively and then move on. This similarity strengthens its relevance to social work. One of the shifts in the approach to project management over the last decade has been to give far more credence to the importance of people management within the process. Being rooted in the construction and engineering industries, historically the focus has been on task completion, but gradually there has been an acceptance that project failures have frequently been related to inattention to the human factors (see Chapter 3). Managing the project processes is equally as important as managing the task completion in securing project success (Bourne and Walker 2004).

Social work model

In social work the processes are complex because people are our business and there are considerable power differentials between those involved. A key factor – and one which singles out the sector – is the centrality of service users to project development (see Chapter 4). To a greater extent than in most other professions, social work recognizes the expertise people have in respect of their needs and constantly strives to reflect this in service development. The benefits of this were seen in Deborah's case study whereby a panel of service users presented Deborah with an alternative way of restructuring her service. Social work needs to pursue a model of project management which reflects the importance of both task and process in its life cycle (Table 5.3).

Table 5.3 Developing a social work dimension to the project life cycle

Task focus (PMI)	Process focus (Tuckman)	Social work focus
Initiating	Forming	Developing the business case, authorizing the project Identification and analysis of stakeholders
Planning	Storming	Defining and refining objectives Stakeholder engagement, managing the power dynamics to produce the best project plan
Executing	Norming	Implementing the plan Developing and enabling collaborative working
Controlling	Performing	Monitoring objectives and performance
Closing	Adjourning	Evaluation, debriefing, managing closure

Limitations of frameworks

One of the shortcomings of frameworks is that in themselves they do not provide a critical analysis of the processes within a project. It is possible to view them as a template, with the expectation that if we follow the stages, complete the tasks and thereby tick all the boxes our project will be successful. Therein lies the rub! The frameworks are not a formula for success. They provide a structure to guide us, but knowing what to do is only part of the conundrum. Knowing how to interpret and use the information we generate and having the skills to manage the processes are equally important.

When we minimize the description of the life cycle to just a few words, it is little wonder that those words struggle to depict the complexity of what is happening as the cycle progresses. This is particularly so in social work and social care in which problems are multi-layered and there is rarely a simple solution. We have already noted that the processes need to be considered and managed with both a task and a people focus, but we also need to be aware that there are two processes that the manager needs to attend to simultaneously.

These are the processes to achieve the *outputs* of the project and the *outcomes*. We have tended to view this as a linear process based on the assumption that if we achieve the outputs then the outcomes will follow. If all goes according to plan then this will be so, but it is not automatic and it is only by skilled management of the processes that this will be accomplished. Let us take Fiona's case study as an example. Senior management requested her to run a series of workshops 'enabling staff to look at research dissemination and providing a forum for highlighting good practice' in order to raise morale. So, the output (the workshops) and the outcome (increased morale) had already been defined. However, Fiona was instantly doubtful as to whether the desired outcome would be realized from that precise output and quickly renegotiated the nature of the workshops. Had she not done this then she would have been left managing two asynchronous processes. Even though she did this, unless she continued to manage the relationship between the two continuously then the outputs could have been tweaked at any time by interested or enthusiastic stakeholders in such a way that they would no longer guarantee the desired outcome. This does not mitigate the need to use a framework to help manage the process, but does highlight its limitations and emphasizes the importance of the project manager retaining a critical eye throughout the life cycle.

Managing from start to finish

The essence of project management has traditionally been seen as managing a balance between budget, time and quality (Martin 2002). As we saw in Chapter 1, in operational management the ongoing nature of the service delivery means that these change and are adjusted over time. In project management they are perceived as being finite and fixed early on in the project, with success being based on the project team's ability to deliver on time, within budget and to the agreed specification. This interrelationship is often illustrated as a triangle with one of the three dimensions depicted at each point. The skill of the project manager is in maintaining control over all three, rather than being a circus plate-spinner with one plate threatening to fall each time too much attention is given to the others.

It has been realized over some years now that even if the project manager does deliver on all three the project may not be deemed a success as one of the key factors in judging success is expectations, that is, the human element, and you will sometimes see the triangle depicted with quality, time and budget representing the three points and expectations in the centre (Horine 2009).

There are models which recognize the need to manage both tasks and people simultaneously. For example, the Classic Six-Stage Project Management Model developed by Elbeik and Thomas (1998) emphasizes the importance of managing, leading and motivating the team throughout the life of the project. In addition to the common project management stages of define, plan, control and review, they argue that team building, leading, motivating and communicating are constant issues running across all of the stages. These aspects of people management and working with stakeholders are the focus of the next chapter. Here we will focus on the tasks that need to be completed while considering the impact of people in relation to these. Although we have defined five stages to the process, these do not have a clear beginning and end. It is easier to think of it as a continuum, so as we are completing one stage we are already beginning the next.

Initiating–planning

Whose idea?

As can be seen from the case studies discussed in Chapter 2, a project can be initiated from anywhere. All three of the case studies described there were designed and implemented as a response to the impact of external factors to some extent – budget cuts, public image and government policy – but the project ideas came from different parts of the organizations.

Deborah's case study showed a team member putting forward a proposal and raised a number of important considerations. Because Deborah's management style is participative and the contributions of team members are valued, the worker's idea was listened to and taken seriously. This might not have happened in every team.

Smale (1998) suggests that not all voices are equal, and that if we reflect on how projects are initiated in our own organizations we will find that they come from a relatively small sector of the workforce, those he refers to as legitimate initiators. This will come as no surprise as we are aware of power dynamics and how these are played out. Whether a person is heard may be affected by how they are perceived due to their gender, ethnicity or level within the hierarchy (Sampson 1999), for example. In respect of project management we cannot afford for this to happen. The hallmark of the project is innovation. To be innovative we need to think differently and those in the most advantageous position to do this are often those whose experiences are different from the norm or who are on the periphery of the 'establishment', so the best ideas for projects can come from anywhere and we need to be open to hearing ideas from wherever they arise.

One of the reasons why people's ideas are dismissed is that they are incomplete because that person does not have access to the 'big picture' within the organization. This could be argued with Deborah's case study. The idea put forward by the worker is based on her experience of working within this and her previous team but does not take account of the wider considerations within the organization, the strategic overview discussed in Chapter 3 – for example it may not make the necessary budget savings, or there may be human resource implications that need to be considered. However, it is vital that ideas are not dismissed prematurely and this just points to the importance of the scoping of the project.

Joined-up planning

The economic and political climate usually presents challenges to social work, but it emphasizes the need to think creatively and differently, which are the ideal pre-determinants of project management. This means:

- planning with realistic optimism – negativity will result in responses such as 'we can't do that because…' or 'we tried that before…'

- creating an ambience which invites service users and staff to generate and put forward suggestions

- ensuring that there is a route through the organization for ideas to be channelled

- detailed scoping of ideas to ensure that they are 'in' or 'out' because they have been thoroughly scrutinized, including testing the assumptions on which they are based.

Testing assumptions

While some voices struggle to be heard, others are viewed as having a perceived wisdom. Clegg *et al.* (2011, p.19) argue that there can be a 'dominant logic' in an organization which acts as a set of blinkers and leads to information being dismissed if it does not conform to senior managers' expectations which are based on habitual thinking. When we receive information we interpret it in order for it to make sense to us and the danger is that we ignore the pieces of information that do not conform to our expectations or we reinterpret the information to make it fit. Part of the process of making sense of something is testing whether it fits with our assumptions. For example, in Fiona's case study an assumption was made that the impact of the inquiry into the death of 17-month-old Peter Connelly (Laming 2009) which had heavily criticized social workers in the authority where Peter lived would be to decrease staff morale even though it did not relate directly to the authority in which Fiona worked. We would probably agree, but it was an assumption that was not proven at the time that the project was initiated. Because it was a widely believed assumption the project was seen as a good idea, but the assumption might have been proved wrong if it were to be tested out. Project proposals based on less widely held assumptions may be dismissed without testing their validity. So, we need to test our assumptions.

Using a Logframe

Project management is renowned for its tool kit, examples of which we have already seen in Chapter 1 – the Project Planning Document and the Project Initiation Document – and Chapter 2 – the PESTLE analysis, SWOT analysis, Force Field analysis and 7S model. Although it would be good to present these to you in a logical format, linking different tools to different phases of the project's development, that is not easily achievable. First of all, many of the tools are not exclusive to project management; and second, all but a few can be used at different stages of the process. One of the advantages is their flexibility and adaptability, so suggesting that their use should be restricted to certain stages would be unhelpful. However, a tool that is particularly helpful at this stage is the Logframe.

This derives from the Logical Framework Approach used in the management of complex international development projects. Through use, several variations of the Logframe have developed, but the differences are minor and the version suggested in Table 5.4 is relevant to social work use.

Table 5.4 Typical structure of a Logframe matrix

Project description	Indicators	Sources of verification	Assumptions
Overall objective – the project's contribution to policy or programme objectives (impact)	How the overall objective will be measured including quantity, quality, time	How the information will be collected, when and by whom	
Purpose – direct benefit to service users (target group)	How the purpose is to be measured including quantity, quality, time	As above	If the purpose is achieved, what assumptions must hold true to achieve the overall objective?
Results – tangible services or products delivered by the project	How the results are to be measured including quantity, quality, time	As above	If results are achieved, what assumptions must hold true to achieve the purpose?
Activities – tasks that have to be undertaken to deliver the desired results			If activities are completed, what assumptions must hold true to deliver the results?

Source: adapted from the European Commission's Project Cycle Management Guidelines, Volume 1 (2004, p.58)

Although the Logframe is introduced here in relation to the initiating stage, you can see that it spans both the initiating and planning stages. By completing this you will test how robust the project idea is and highlight serious flaws in thinking. There are some assumptions, better known as 'killer assumptions', that will jeopardize the success of the project if they do not hold true, so their early identification is essential. For example, the move towards personalized budgets is based on an assumption that people want control over their finances, independence of choice and responsibility for their decisions. This may be true for the majority of people, but unless the assumption holds true for everyone, a project based on this premise will fail if it happens to be for the minority who do not want this.

The 'On the Spot' activity in Box 5.1 is an exercise in completing a Logframe matrix for yourself.

Box 5.1

'On the Spot' – Analysing our assumptions

Using either a project of your own as an example or one of the three case studies in Chapter 2, complete a Logframe matrix. The assumptions may not always be easy to identify as they are sometimes based on 'taken for granted' ways of thinking.

Key reflection points

Completing the Logframe should help you to:

- identify the evidence for knowledge, information, beliefs and assumptions

- make clear links between what we do and what is achieved from what we do

- demonstrate that attention is paid to balancing time and resources with quality.

At this early stage a PESTLE analysis (see Fiona's case study) or the 7S model (see Deborah's case study) can also be useful as scoping tools. These will help with the early identification of potential risk factors, which will need to run throughout the project and is explored in some detail in Chapter 7.

Planning–executing

The planning stage was outlined in Chapter 1 and is essentially the answer to what, why, where, who and when. This takes the form of a project definition or project initiation document:

- *What* – defining the project, the outputs and outcomes and any problems anticipated in their achievement.

- *Why* – the business case.

- *Where* – the journey from beginning to end of the project.

- *Who* – the project team, service users, partners, funders.

- *When* – the timescale.

There are different format suggestions for this document, the key consideration being that it is a working document; it will be your working manual and needs to include the information that will aid your management of the project. So, some detail needs to be determined by the individual project but it needs to provide a reference point to keep the project on track and address difficulties that are encountered along the way.

To do this it needs to provide clarity and specificity, so it needs to be more than a statement of intent. While the Logframe is useful to test out the premise of the project, the initiation document turns that premise into reality by demonstrating precisely how the idea will come to fruition.

To make this a 'living' document it is important that it is owned by all concerned in the process, so they should be involved in its production to as great an extent as possible. This can prove difficult because until the business case has been accepted there probably will not be a project team. As we will see in the next chapter, people's involvement evolves as the project progresses, with some becoming more involved and others becoming less involved. So, the idea of producing a document at the beginning of the project which will hold true for its duration may be less relevant in service development than in product development.

On the one hand we need to be exact about some of the detail of the project in order to know that it will work, while on the other hand maintaining a dialogic process so that stakeholders (see Chapter 4) can contribute and feel engaged with the project, keeping in mind that this is also the stage where competing expectations are likely to surface. The art then is in identifying the most appropriate point for each element of the initiation document to become fixed, recognizing what is non-negotiable from an early stage and what needs to reach maturity through deliberation.

As we saw from the case studies, projects do not always emerge in the neat logical ways that we might hope for. In Fiona's case the outputs and outcomes were set before resource implications had been identified, while in Deborah's the project had to save money rather than spend it, so the project costs had to be set against projected savings. This is the real world, and rapid, emergent change will precipitate spontaneous project developments which may evolve erratically. One of the roles of the project manager is to bring the project under control in these early stages, and this involves scheduling, which is explored below.

Executing–controlling

Simple scheduling

Scheduling is an excellent way of helping to identify the costs of the project – so some scheduling may be done in the initial stages – but also of managing the implementation and demonstrating control. Simple scheduling can take the form of a list in the order that tasks need to be completed, if the order matters. Some of us do this all of the time in our everyday lives, although we are not all 'list' people. For example, when planning your weekend itinerary you will probably try to design it so that you manage all your shopping in one journey rather than travelling into town three or four times. Some of us (so we are led to believe) even write our shopping lists in the order that we will pass the items in the supermarket so as to shorten the route. This sort of planning is aimed at achieving efficiency. The tasks are not interdependent, so although it might take longer to complete, there are no dire consequences if we have to go back through a few aisles before we collect all of our items. Time is of the essence, though, in project management, so even this very simple type of scheduling is important. It can also be useful for managing the budget – if we make a list before we go to the supermarket and stick to it we are likely to spend less and also have the opportunity to cross items off the list that we would like but cannot afford. The same argument holds true in project management.

Sequential and parallel scheduling

However, often the achievement of one task impacts on others. For example:

> Julie is due to meet the architect and builder at 10.00 hours at the construction site for renovation of the care home she is overseeing. She has some important questions that she needs answers to about time scales, construction site traffic and the environmental impact of the work as she has a press release to prepare later in the day and is meeting with people from the local community that evening. The building manager has to cancel at short notice in order to deal with an emergency at another site, and although she still meets with the architect he deflects most of the questions as they are in the building manager's domain.

Julie is now in the unenviable position of having to write the press release and meet important stakeholders without the detailed information she needs. She is still able to complete her tasks, but not to the standard she had hoped. With hindsight, scheduling events so closely together which impact on each other may not have been the best planning. However, we cannot always allow time for slippage between events, so if Julie has planned her schedule she will have a contingency plan:

> When she saw that all three events were going to be scheduled for the same day Julie was concerned about the consequences of something going wrong. So she emailed her questions to the architect and building manager two days before the meeting was due, asking for a discussion of the issues when they met. On the morning of the meeting when the building manager couldn't attend he agreed to email her some information from his phone when he arrived at the other site and they'd reconvene the meeting at the earliest date. Not ideal, but her forward planning meant that Julie had enough information to be able to write a good press release and have an honest discussion with local people later that day.

In project management scheduling enables us to:

- control project costs
- make efficient use of time
- identify interdependencies between tasks
- identify tasks and occurrences which are outside of our control
- anticipate problems and delays
- devise a contingency plan
- achieve our objectives.

Scheduling tools offer different levels of simplicity and sophistication, and one of the most popular ones is illustrated here. The Gantt chart is a quick and easy way of beginning to schedule which is very visual and can be a constant reminder of what is meant to happen when. On one axis all of the tasks are identified and the other axis maps the timescale. Within this you can note the earliest start date, the estimated duration, which tasks are sequential and which can run in parallel, and which are dependent on the completion of other tasks.

The example in Table 5.5 is brief and simple but illustrates how a Gantt chart can be used to manage time and identify the potential impact each stage might have. If the drop-in members decide that a street party is not how they want to celebrate, the project stops there. If the neighbours object, the application to the council and the application for funding are considerably weakened.

Table 5.5 Gantt chart example

Initial planning of a community street party to celebrate the 25th anniversary of a drop-in centre for people with learning disabilities				
Task	Earliest start date	Duration	Sequential or parallel	Dependent on
A. Consultation with drop-in members	Week 0	Ongoing	S	
B. Consultation with neighbours	Week 1	1–2 weeks	S	A
C. Establish planning group	Week 1	Ongoing	S	A
D. Apply to local council for agreement	Week 3	3 months	P	A, B, C
E. Make business case to secure funding	Week 3	2 weeks	P	A, B, C

The difference between parallel and sequential tasks is particularly important to examine. Sequential tasks may have a much more serious impact on the project than just the time by which they overrun. For example, if a report is produced a day late and is to be presented to an authorizing body which only meets monthly, the consequence of that task overrunning by one day will have the potential impact of a one-month delay on the overall project. With this in mind, the project manager needs to prioritize tasks carefully and identify alternative sequences which will minimize the impact of the delay. So, in this situation the manager could schedule the writing of the report to be completed several days before the committee meeting, reducing the cost of slippage, or they could rearrange the sequence of other tasks to ensure that the person writing the report has no other competing demands that would prevent the report being completed on time.

A key determinant of success during this stage is being crystal clear about who is responsible for the completion of what. This is not about engendering a culture of blame, but if you have managed any group work previously you will be aware of the potential for misunderstanding and disagreement in relation to this. This is explored in more detail in Chapters 6 and 7, but is flagged here as a prompt to make sure you consider it.

In Box 5.2, you are asked to prepare a Gantt chart for a piece of work you are currently involved in.

Box 5.2

'On the Spot' – Scheduling

Consider a piece of work you are currently involved in which has a clear end date. Prepare a Gantt chart in relation to the work and then identify:

- the critical stages of the process

- what is success dependent on – for example, is it allocation of resources or other people completing tasks?

Finally, consider whether you can develop a contingency plan to ensure you are able to complete your work in time and to the standard expected.

If you look at your completed Gantt chart you should be able to identify the shortest route from the beginning to end for your work, but at the same time observe any events that might cause problematic delays. We cannot always avoid problems but we can minimize their impact if we are prepared for them and try to work round them rather than just being determined they won't happen.

Controlling–closing

If you have followed the process so far, then you should be well on your way to completing your project successfully. Your outcomes were agreed in your Logframe, the deliverables formed part of your business case, you have monitored and controlled your budget and ensured that you can complete on time through your scheduling. However, in the real world of project management that is not always going to be the case of course. You have to expect the unexpected, pre-empt what you can and respond quickly to what you cannot.

Impact on the team

As you will see in the next chapter, the impact of those involved in the project can be critical at this stage as they begin to disengage and move on to their next venture, and it can feel like a lonely place for the project manager to be. It will be you who is ultimately accountable for delivery, and your team's responsibilities are likely to end before yours as you dot the 'i's', cross the 't's' and generally clear up the aftermath. This final stage will vary according to the nature of the project and its impact. Whether it is leading on to a positive service development or terminating an existing service, for example, will influence the emotional effect, but inevitably there will be elements of happiness and sadness as the project draws to an end and this will be different for each individual involved in the project.

Paying attention to individuals is a must, ensuring closure not just for the project but for them too. The ending may be marked by dissemination events, which are a good way of ensuring people are thanked for their contribution and feel valued, but the ending can be an anticlimax leaving people feeling slightly empty, or so hurried because the next project is about to start that they do not have the opportunity to reflect on the experience and hopefully revel in their success.

Rather than considering tools, methods or applications at this stage the project manager needs to use her or his people skills to the maximum to be able to tune in to how the ending is for each person, debrief and help them to move on.

Chapter summary

During this chapter we have looked at the process of a project from beginning to end and highlighted the key considerations at each of the different stages. As we have seen, there are a range of tools which can be helpful in managing the practical tasks of the project, with a particular emphasis on planning, scheduling and sequencing tasks effectively. In Chapter 6 we will move on to considering the human elements of project management – engaging stakeholders and managing the project team.

Action checklist

When embarking on a project:

- Map the anticipated life cycle of your project at the earliest opportunity.

- Identify the tools which will assist you, such as the Project Planning Document, Project Initiation Document, PESTLE analysis, SWOT analysis, Force Field analysis, 7S model, Logframe matrix or Gantt chart.

- Ensure you are managing tasks and processes simultaneously.

- Plan a positive ending.

Chapter 6

Leading Your Project Team and Developing Partnerships

Introduction

Few managers in social work will have ever identified that they want to be a project manager, but increasingly they are likely to take on this role at some point in their career. The phrase 'accidental project manager' (Graham 1992) has been coined quite aptly in relation to public sector project managers because while in construction or engineering, for example, 'project management' is a job that people choose to go into, in the public sector, including social work, it is a position that you just find yourself in and might be wondering, 'How did that happen?' As was highlighted in Chapter 3, one of the most common reasons for using project management in social work is to introduce change, and as change becomes increasingly rapid and complex so too does the use of a project management approach. The key question we will be attempting to answer in this chapter is, 'What do I need to do differently as a project manager?' This chapter looks specifically at the influence that stakeholders will have on your project and discusses how you might adapt your own leadership style to manage your project stakeholders. Skills in motivation are essential to facilitate your team to work productively together.

What skills does a project manager need?

Bourne and Walker (2004) suggest that the skills needed by the project manager can be differentiated into three tiers:

- *Tier 1.* Managing the open issues – these relate to task management that we looked at in the last chapter.

- *Tier 2.* Managing the under-the-table issues – these relate to managing the dynamics of how the people work together.

- *Tier 3.* Managing the emerging issues – these are the political issues and agendas that influence the direction and progress of the project.

One of the key skills in relation to tier 1 is decision-making. We have already seen the process which the manager has to direct and some of the tools that can be useful, but the manager is constantly making decisions to take the project from initiation to closure. We will explore decision-making more in the next chapter when we consider risk management, but the focus in this chapter is on tiers 2 and 3 – how to manage the impact of people on the project. First we will explore stakeholder management, which was introduced in Chapter 1, followed by team management, and will consider the role the project manager plays in relation to each.

Stakeholder management

'Stakeholder' is a fairly common term, and one of the clearest definitions is 'any group or individual who can affect or is affected by the achievement of the organisation's objectives' (Freeman 1984, p.46). Potentially this refers to a sizeable group, and if you consider the work you are involved in and apply this definition it may be a very wide group including politicians, some members of the public, local organizations and the media as well as those you are providing a service for, your team and those you work in partnership or collaboratively with. As public sector workers we have a duty not only to ourselves and our team but to our employer, which will be evident in organizational policies and our employment contract, to service users and to the public set down in government policies. How we carry out our duties will be monitored by politicians and the press, who think that they have the public's interests at heart. The expectations and requirements of these groups frequently clash and those which are most important are not always most influential.

One of the most common causes of project failure is lack of effective engagement with stakeholders (OGC 2005) and it is now widely accepted that stakeholder management is an essential component of the project manager's role (Assudani and Kloppenborg 2010; McElroy and Mills 2003). If carried out effectively it will help to build trust and ownership of the project and decrease the amount of conflict between stakeholders (Chigona et al. 2010). There used to be a widely held belief that, provided a project was completed on time, on budget and produced the agreed output, it would be deemed to be a success. Experience has proved this to be a flawed argument and it is now recognized that stakeholder satisfaction is a major success criterion. The nature of social care work – a people-intensive industry – which is there to serve everyone as the need arises, has an extensive span of influence which brings with it substantial stakeholder interest. Managing stakeholder expectations is, therefore, one of the biggest challenges of project management in this sector.

Step 1 – Where to begin

You will recall from Chapter 5 that we highlighted the tension that can exist between making key decisions early on in the project life and involving stakeholders and team members in those decisions. One way of thinking of the project life cycle is as either deliberate or emergent (Assudani and Kloppenborg 2010). There are some projects where a clearly defined outcome will be identified from the start (i.e. deliberate), and others which may be exploratory or the outcomes may change in light of the dialogue with stakeholders and possible external developments (i.e. emergent). This difference is critical to determining how to manage stakeholder expectations.

This should be viewed as a continuum rather than trying to identify a project as either deliberate or emergent, but pinpointing it on the continuum will help you to define the process that should follow (Figure 6.1). At one end of the continuum will be projects where the outcomes are already clearly defined and there is minimum room for negotiation on inputs or process. In these situations the relationship with stakeholders will need to be marked by clear and effective engagement and communication, ensuring that they know what to expect, how and when.

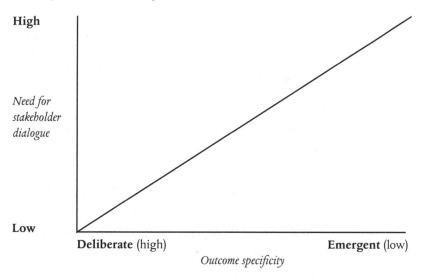

Figure 6.1 Deliberate–emergent continuum

Source: based on the work of Assundani and Kloppenborg (2010)

As we travel along the continuum and the project becomes less clearly defined, the relationship with stakeholders will change significantly, becoming more consultative and dialogic. Reflecting on Deborah's case study (see Chapter 2), one of the outcomes – saving 15 per cent – was deliberate and non-negotiable, but what outputs needed to be produced in order to achieve this had not been defined. Deborah was able to enter into dialogue with the team and with service users and ideas emerged from this process.

Step 2 – Stakeholder analysis

Stakeholder analysis is a popular project management technique and a useful exercise to help you as the project manager to understand the range and intensity of influence that different stakeholders have at the beginning of the process of engagement. It has its limitations because stakeholders are human and as such do not always behave rationally, logically or predictably, so their expectations, agenda and influence may change during the life cycle of the project. Also it classifies people as a homogeneous group and, while some of their views and influence may result from membership of their group, individuals may also have personal views and power which become evident at different stages of the project life cycle. It is, however, a practical way of beginning to map out and understand the location of the project at its inception.

- To begin your analysis list the different groups of stakeholders who have an interest in or are affected by your project. Building on previous work (Li 2007; Walker, Bourne and Rowlinson 2008), Rowlinson and Cheung (2008) have developed a useful classification for stakeholders:

  - *Upstream stakeholders* – users or recipients of the service being developed.

  - *Downstream stakeholders* – those who will be providing resources and services to the project team to enable them to develop the service.

  - *External stakeholders* – those with a vested interest or who might be affected by the development of the service, for example neighbours and local community groups.

  - *Invisible stakeholders* – those who will work with or influence the project delivery team, for example professional partner groups.

- ○ *Project stakeholder group* – those who commissioned the project and the project delivery team.

- Then make a note of their agenda – what would constitute project success to each group. This may include groups who are opposing the project.

- Next, assess their level of influence in respect of the project, that is, the extent to which they are in a position of power or have access to those who are. One suggestion (Kloppenborg 2009) is to identify them by the nature of their influence – whether they can positively or negatively influence or be influenced by the project process or results.

Step 3 – Defining the relationship
Approaches to conflict and uncertainty

What you do with the results of your stakeholder analysis will need to take account of the nature of the project (the deliberate–emergent continuum), and your analysis will help you to determine the best way forward. You need to be aware, though, as a manager you will have a preferred style of how to work in this situation which will impact on your decisions at this point. Koppenjan and Klijn (2004) suggest that managers respond differently when dealing with uncertainty. Some will want to find the shortest route to restoring certainty, whilst others will see the potential for new and emerging ideas to emanate from the uncertainty.

'DISENTANGLERS'

Koppenjan and Klijn refer to the first group as 'disentanglers' as they aim to simplify the situation by reaching a decision about what will happen next as quickly as possible. Their discomfort with uncertainty is likely to influence how they perceive the differing views of stakeholders – as either 'for' or 'against' – and their approach will be to root out the opposition.

'ENTANGLERS'

The second group is referred to as 'entanglers' as they see the differing views as the start of a process which will enable a better outcome to be achieved. They question and debate the ideas to gain a fuller understanding and aim to ensure that the best option is taken forward. In Claire's experience (see Chapter 4), we saw how she acted as an entangler, commissioning the Alzheimer's Society to find out the views of a hundred service users and carers so that she could see the 'bigger picture'. As both complimentary and critical views emerged from this process it 'created the foundations for all agencies to find solutions together to some of the shortcomings in local provision'.

Impact of preferred approach

The significance of this is that we each need to know our own preferred approach to uncertainty, and we will be able to identify this quite easily if we reflect honestly on our past experience. Then we need to match our approach to the different types of project on our deliberate–emergent continuum. If you look again at the continuum you will see that a project at the 'deliberate' end of the continuum will require a management approach which is decisive. There is little room for negotiation; the key role of the project manager is to drive forward the project as designed and a 'disentangler' would be able to do this effectively. There are, however, few projects that are situated at the extreme deliberate end of the continuum. As we travel along the continuum the need for an 'entangler' emerges, as the pivotal role of the manager is to draw out the differing expectations of the stakeholders to develop the best outcomes for the project. The manager will need to engage with stakeholders and manage their expectations in the early part of the project life cycle, but how these are managed and the degree to which this will be an integral, ongoing aspect of the project will vary between deliberate and emergent projects.

As a social work project manager you need to be able to adapt your style to suit the needs of the project. It is quite possible that you will be involved in managing more than one project at a time and they may require different approaches, so it is critical for you to be able to identify and question your approach to uncertainty in relation to each project.

Step 4 – Working with stakeholders

We need to communicate effectively with stakeholders, but how to achieve this will vary from project to project. Assudani and Kloppenborg (2010, p.68) suggest social network theory has relevance to managing ongoing relationships as it 'examines the interaction among people that are integrally involved at various phases of the process'.

Social network theory uses the terms 'nodes' and 'ties', nodes being the individual stakeholders and ties being the connections between them, and the process is simply to map these out. As we saw from Colin's experience (see Chapter 4), service users are not only involved in one project in a lifetime, but they may be involved in many, developing networks and expertise as they go. The advantage of using this theory is that it recognizes the stakeholders as individuals, providing a more sophisticated analysis, and so it identifies the key players. From this the project manager can determine how to influence and manage relationships for the benefit of the project. This will be an ongoing process rather than a one-off activity and you can adapt your approach as the dynamics evolve.

Another important factor to consider, though, is the type of communication and relationship that might be needed with different stakeholders at various points of the project cycle. As we have seen, not all will have the same interest in or influence regarding the project, and this will be affected by the stage the project is at. Chigona *et al.* (2010) have identified four types of relationship that might be relevant:

- inform
- consult
- partnership
- control.

They suggest that these should be mapped for each stakeholder group at different life cycle stages. In social work the term 'partnership' is used to describe a wide variety of working relationships. 'Collaborative' and 'integrated' have also become well-used terms, but none of these communicate effectively the distinct nature of specific working arrangements. One of the strengths of Chigona *et al.*'s approach is that it encourages us to assess those relationships and be more exact in determining the course of their development.

Previous work (Miller, Whoriskey and Cook 2008; Petch, Cook and Miller 2005) has indicated a dissonance between the outcomes service users want and the outcomes determined by partnerships, so it is crucial that, within the stakeholder arena, working relationships are established which enable the priorities of service users to be recognized and maintained throughout the project cycle. We saw in Claire's account how she utilized different approaches to consultation with different groups of stakeholders at different stages of the process. She commissioned detailed research regarding the views of service users and carers, conducted a 'public engagement' exercise to gather the views of other interested groups which led to the production of a report and then at the next stage established a Strategic Commissioning Group which comprised service users and service providers with knowledge, expertise, drive and a sense of responsibility to take the issues forward. This illustrates how to manage stakeholder involvement effectively to achieve the best results for the project.

Take a look at the 'On the Spot' exercise in Box 6.1. From your stakeholder map you will be able to manage your relationships. If you considered Deborah's case study, for example, you will have taken account of the unique position of her team within the borough – that is, it is funded differently and provides a borough-wide service – which may affect how other professionals view the service. Her team offers a service which does not always attract sympathetic treatment from the media and the public, which also needs to be recognized. As you work through your project the nature and purpose of your communication with each stakeholder group will be clear and will ensure that you pitch their involvement at the most appropriate level.

Box 6.1

'On the Spot' – Stakeholder mapping

Using either one of the case studies in Chapter 2 or an example of your own:

1. Map the stakeholders.

2. Identify the nature and intensity of their influence as you perceive it.

3. Identify whether this is a positive or negative influence.

4. Map any links that exist between stakeholder groups so that you can see how levels of influence may change.

5. Now consider the type of relationship you would consider most appropriate for each group: inform, consult, partnership or control.

Networking

The key skills the project manager will use in relation to engaging and managing stakeholder expectations are networking and boundary spanning. Networking can happen at an individual, community, organizational and inter-organizational level (Banks *et al.* 2003; McKimm and Phillips 2009), and if you have experience at any level you will have an insight into the skills involved. One of the challenges of networking is sustainability. Most of us are motivated and able to make contact with others when we can see the direct result that can be achieved from that contact, but we know from our everyday lives how easy it is to lose touch with people when we are busy – another week, month or year goes by without making the call, not because we don't want to but because it gets overtaken by other more pressing priorities. People who are good networkers will make the call in spite of those other priorities. They have the ability to prioritize activities that may not have a direct or immediate result – they understand the accumulative value of all of those calls and therefore allocate them much greater priority.

There may be a link between networking and Rogers' 'Innovations Curve' (1995) whereby he suggests that those who are more ready to adapt to new practices tend to be those with wider networks who have a greater awareness of professional developments. Dodgeson and Rothwell (1994) note that networking appears to be increasingly necessary for innovation; but while a proclivity towards networking may be useful regarding sustainability, the challenge of developing effective networks is both skilled and strategic (Gilchrist 2000).

Working with uncertainty

A key aspect of this is being able to work with uncertainty as 'roles, identities and meanings are constantly being interpreted and renegotiated' (McKimm and Phillips 2009, p.65). Those roles may include broker, mediator, advocate and interpreter within an environment of misunderstanding (Gilchrist 2000). Klijn *et al.* (2008) note a differentiation between project management and process/network management in some of the literature (e.g. Kickert, Klijn and Koppenjan 1997; Meredith and Mantel 2000). They suggest that there is an important tension between the two as project management has traditionally been seen as 'goal realization' while process/ network management involves 'goal searching', as to some degree it is an iterative process which needs to respond to stakeholders' needs as they emerge. This supports the previous work by Koppenjan and Klijn (2004) regarding disentanglers and entanglers that we considered earlier in the chapter.

As Pinto (2000) argues, projects will be perceived by some as a threat, and whether or not the perception is legitimate it is real and needs to be addressed, so the project manager needs to be able to embrace political behaviour by being sensitive to the threats, negotiating, bargaining and compromising as necessary to achieve the success of the project. Keys and

Case (1990) provide a useful checklist to ongoing success in influencing others:

- Ensure you know your subject well – when you talk about your project your credibility will initially be determined largely by the level of expertise you display.

- Reflect on your relationships – prioritize those which are linked to your project rather than people you contact through habit or preference.

- Check whether you need to develop your network to include people with specific expertise or resources that will assist you in your project.

- Think carefully about how you approach people and the nature of your contact.

- Show sensitivity and flexibility in your contact and communicate clearly.

Developing trust

A key aspect of networking that warrants emphasis is the development of trust (Banks *et al.* 2003; Gilchrist 2000; McKimm and Phillips 2009; Newell and Swan 2000). Within the literature there are different arguments about the nature and development of trust, and Newell and Swan have suggested the following typology:

- companion trust based on goodwill or friendship

- competence trust based on level of expertise

- commitment trust based on a formal agreement to work together.

It is important to be able to analyse the nature of the trust you develop within your network and recognise its basis in order to avoid misunderstandings, disappointments and potential for conflict.

Boundary spanning

Boundary spanning encompasses the skills and processes of networking and more besides. A cautionary note expressed about networking is that it can blur boundaries. At an individual level it is approached as a social activity, and without a clear focus the search for commonalities between the parties involved can undermine existing loyalties and relationships. The boundary spanner has a more demarcated approach, which is essential to success as it is a 'balancing act between inclusion and separation, dependence and autonomy' (Williams 2002, p.111). The boundary spanner is not appointed to the role, indeed it is not a formal role, but it is a term that has become associated with people who enable partnerships to work effectively by informally influencing the dynamics and working relationships between the different partners to enable the group to achieve its goals.

Because the project manager is in a formal position there are some differences between the two roles, but the lack of organizational power assigned to some project managers highlights the need for them to be proficient in boundary spanning skills.

Boundary spanning skills

Williams (2002) identified through his research a number of strengths associated with the boundary spanner: the ability to build sustainable relationships, manage through influencing and negotiation, manage complexity and interdependencies, and manage roles, accountabilities and motivations.

The skills allied to these areas of practice include:

- communicating clearly

- using terminology that is empowering to all

- developing relationships that can withstand disagreement and conflict

- demonstrating integrity, approachability and tolerance

- translating strategy into practice, which includes balancing different agendas, defining roles and responsibilities, negotiating agreements and evaluating outcomes

- managing multiple accountabilities.

Developing the project team

'The most successful projects are characterized by having had a well-considered and well-developed plan and an outstanding, committed team' (Thomas et al. 2008, p.105). The particular challenges to developing such a team for a project manager were highlighted in Chapter 1 and included:

- In some projects the team will have been co-opted from other teams to which they will return at the end of the project. This will impact on loyalties and commitment and the workers may continue to be 'line managed' by their originating team manager.

- The project manager may not have been involved in the selection of the project team. While this is the situation for any manager new to a team, in project work there is limited time for getting to know the team or identifying their strengths and development needs.

- The team will need to work differently from a service delivery team.

- Workers attracted to being part of a project team are more likely to welcome change and innovation, which will be useful in driving the work forward, but they are likely to lack skills in other areas as a result.

- The priorities and approach of a project manager will need to be different from those of an operational manager.

- Team members who have not worked on a project team previously or who know you in a different management role may find the adjustment testing.

- Team members may have their own agenda in joining the project in relation to their career aspirations.

- Members may begin to leave as the end of the project nears.

- The team is not intended to survive long-term. It exists to achieve a particular outcome and then be dismantled. This will affect team processes and the project manager needs to be skilled at managing endings well.

While social work has become more outcome-focused project management has become more process-focused, and achieving a balance between these two and the relationship between them are critical.

Working together?

One of the questions to ask yourself is, 'How will I know if the team is working effectively?' It has been argued (Ding and Ding 2008) that there is a tendency with regard to group working to evaluate only the end product, that is, whether the project has achieved its outcomes, and much more emphasis needs to be placed on evaluating the way in which teams have worked together in order to achieve the end product as this will result in a much more effective and productive team. In suggesting this they are commenting particularly on the idea known as 'free-riding' whereby a group member shares in the success of the whole group while contributing little individually.

If you were to ask each of your team members if they have ever experienced free-riding in a group they have worked with, they are very likely to say 'yes', but if you ask them what the group leader or manager did about it they will probably say 'nothing'. Also known as 'social loafing' (Adams and Anantatmula 2010; Latane, Williams and Harkins 1979), this phenomenon is common in group working, so has been experienced by many of us, and yet there is a tendency for it to be accommodated rather than challenged. Otherwise assertive, articulate people allow themselves to be manoeuvred into doing more than a fair share of the work and those in charge allow it to happen – why?

The process of free-riding survives because of particular circumstances which are usually evident in project work:

- The emphasis is on outcome rather than process – in a target-driven culture is a manager likely to be overly concerned who did what if the outcome has been achieved?

- Loyalty of group members – generally no-one wants to report or complain about another team member to their manager.

- Fear of losing control – if other team members cover the work of the free-rider they remain in control of what is happening. If they report it or make waves within the group to try to address it they don't know what will happen.

- Skills of the free-rider – sometimes the free-rider is not particularly skilled at behaving this way – it may be a one-off experience due to pressures in other aspects of their life – but more often it is practised behaviour which they have become quite adept at. They will have a repertoire of techniques for shifting responsibility for work from themselves to others and may appear to be very helpful – offering to take on a range of tasks, but never actually being free when the tasks need completing!

- Group mood – if the project is going well and there is a positive group mood individuals are likely to volunteer to do more (Adams and Anantatmula 2010; George 1991).

- Commitment to the project – the overriding concern of most of the group members will be completion of the project, and if that involves taking on more than a fair share of the work then they are usually willing to do it.

Traditional ways of working and managing in social work (i.e. one-to-one) do not lend themselves readily to developing team working – a manager may have little opportunity to observe the team working as a team, supervision may focus on the individual rather than the team and targets are likely to be established through an individual appraisal process. This is a key reason why it may be useful to think about working differently when project managing.

Group or team?

The key difference between a group and a team is that the goals of team members are interdependent (Parker 2006; West and Markiewicz 2004). This is always the case in project management but may not have been so in the previous experience of the team members. In social and health care services team members are often used to working alongside and with others but can achieve their targets independently of other team members. This is particularly so when staff have case responsibility, for example in physiotherapy, occupational therapy and social work. Not only is it essential to transform the project members into a team but also time is of the essence.

Coaching

West and Markiewicz (2004) suggest that this requires a different style of management, one in which the manager takes on the role of the coach, ensuring that the team has the resources, skills and a positive environment in which to work effectively together. A team which recognizes its interdependency will contribute to ensuring that individual members are supported and will carry out this function on a day-to-day basis. The project manager therefore needs to consider carefully the nature and style of his/ her interaction and intervention with team members in order to nurture and promote this interdependency and mutual support.

There are various models of coaching, but the one mentioned here has most in common with sports coaching, in which the importance of the balance between process and outcome is keenly observed. If a team achieves a comfortable win the sports coach will still look at the individual performance of each player as well as how they performed together. The fact that they won will not be seen as a reason not to address free-riding!

To achieve the goal of 'an outstanding, committed team' everyone needs to be performing to their optimum potential, but we have already highlighted that in a project team members may be inhibited from doing this because they have divided loyalties, may not have all of the necessary skills and may have a personal agenda. This is unavoidable; what is important is how the manager responds to it.

In sports coaching it is recognized that what is going on inside a person will affect how they perform on the outside. If we want to improve the performance then we have to address what is happening mentally or emotionally for that person (Gallwey 2000). Whatever is preventing the person maximizing their performance is seen as interference and it is the role of the coach to reduce it as much as possible (Downey 2003). Interference may be boredom, lack of confidence, anger or other states of mind which prevent the person focusing on the goal. Similarly, in project management it is the manager's role to identify what is preventing the team performing at their best.

Coaching the team to excellence

We have already noted, in Chapter 5, the relevance of Tuckman's (1965) group development process to the stages of the project life cycle. Adams and Anantatmula (2010) have suggested a useful taxonomy of the stages of social and behavioural development which is closely aligned with Tuckman's model. They argue that when an individual first joins a group or team their preoccupation is self, but as the group develops they focus more on a shared agenda. The five stages of evolution are:

- *Self-identity.* The focus of the individual is self.

- *Social identity.* The individual team members begin to influence each other.

- *Group emotion.* Individual emotions can be assumed by the group, giving them a perception of greater importance.

- *Group mood* – this is an extension of group emotion. While emotions may be fleeting, group mood lasts longer and is therefore more pervasive.

- *Emotional intelligence.* Complete trust is established within the group.

The style of the project manager needs to adapt as the project team develops through these stages. At the beginning the manager needs to focus on the individuals within the team, assessing their skills and demonstrating assertive leadership to set the working parameters. This style will become less directive as the team develops. By the final stage of emotional intelligence the team is effectively managing itself and the manager is intervening only to keep them on track, encourage creativity and remove any barriers to achieving their outcomes.

Two features of project teams which can be particularly challenging are:

- They may be multi-disciplinary or multi-professional, as team members may have been seconded from other teams and organizations for the purpose of the project.

- They are time-limited.

Edmondson and Nembhard (2009, p.125) comment on the importance of creating 'psychological safety' in project teams in order that team members will feel able to share ideas which may be embryonic. This can feel personally risky and individuals are unlikely to take that step if they feel vulnerable or unconfident, but it is essential that this sharing takes place in order that creativity and innovation are encouraged and the best outcomes can be achieved. The risks involved in this process are heightened by the potential threat of being misunderstood by those from other disciplines. Time helps, as the sense of team security will increase as they successfully navigate the stages of group development, but the clock is ticking and in short-term projects they may not reach the stage of emotional intelligence unless the project manager takes action to increase the pace of development.

In these circumstances the role of the project manager may appear unenviable and achievement of a committed and outstanding team idealistic, but by adapting their style to recognize the different needs of a project team success is attainable. Here are a few tips:

- Ensure that the development of the project team and the project plan go hand-in-hand. This means being able to work with uncertainty and requires skills in nurturing and guiding the team in the early stages of development, but will result in a much stronger commitment to the plan from them.

- Make sure that each team member is clear about their role, understands what is expected of them and has the skills to fulfil their role.

- Spend time getting to know the individual strengths of each team member and observing how they work with each other. Compatibility and difference both have their place in project development. The skill is in knowing when and how to deploy them in the project cycle.

- Encourage the team to use a responsibility matrix. This involves them taking ownership of task completion. It avoids misunderstandings, ensures fairness and transparency of workloads and thereby increases 'buy-in' from individuals to the team approach.

- Build in regular reviews which require specific comment on progress to date and involve the team in supporting each other and finding solutions to unforeseen problems and barriers.

- Develop ground rules for discussion and encourage debate of diverse approaches and options.

- Seek feedback from the team about your own style and be prepared to adapt.

Emotional intelligence

The key skills involved in managing a project team rather than an operational team are, in summary, a greater awareness of self and others. In order to be able to respond quickly, identify strengths, manage tensions and conflicts and still achieve in relation to time, budget and quality, the project manager needs to be perceptive, understand his/her own approaches and how these impact on others, and manage team strengths and dynamics. This highlights the significance of the project manager being emotionally aware. Whilst literature in respect of emotionally intelligent leadership is replete, the study by Clarke (2010) is the first to determine a relationship between project manager competence in teamwork and managing conflicts and emotional intelligence. Mayer and Salovey (1997) identified four dimensions to emotional intelligence, defining it as the ability to:

1. perceive accurately, appraise, and express emotions

2. access and/or generate feelings when they facilitate thought

3. understand emotion and emotional knowledge

4. regulate emotions to promote emotional and intellectual growth.

Druskat and Druskat (2006) have suggested four aspects of project management wherein emotional intelligence is particularly relevant:

1. The development of trust and commitment, given the temporary nature of the project.

2. The development of relationships that will result in a greater sharing of knowledge. As each project has unique elements this can be an important contributor to a project's success.

3. The ability to motivate the team through complex change processes.

4. The ability to manage conflict.

Previous studies, such as Dulewicz and Higgs (2003), had argued that the leadership competencies of emotional resilience and communication contributed to the success of projects which were of medium complexity while the competency of sensitivity contributed to the success of highly complex projects. Sunindijo, Hadikusumo and Ogunlana (2007) found that project managers with higher levels of emotional intelligence demonstrated key leadership behaviours such as proactivity, leading by example, rewarding and good communication skills.

Clarke's (2010) work highlights the significance of the project manager's ability to 'access and generate feelings when they facilitate thought' (Mayer and Salovey 1997, p.10) and the contribution this makes to effective teamwork and the ability to manage conflict. He also found a link between empathy and attentiveness resulting in project managers who have a high level of empathy demonstrating the ability to develop strong, responsive and productive relationships. Whether and/or the degree to which emotional intelligence can be developed is highly contested and Mayer and Salovey's definition emphasizes its complexity. However, there is support for the view that it can be developed within an organizational context (Clarke 2006; Moriarty and Buckley 2003). If we view emotional intelligence as a continuum from low to high we are all on there somewhere, and while we may never progress to the highest levels we can adopt practices which will maintain and develop our awareness of and emotional responses to ourself and others.

Improving our awareness

A tool that can be quite useful in achieving this is de Bono's PMI exercise. PMI stands for Plus, Minus and Interesting and is a scanning tool to assist us in seeing the different perspectives of a situation. It might, at first glance, seem similar to SWOT and PESTLE (illustrated in the case studies in Chapter 2) but those are analytical tools, and if you undertake them as a group you should find it possible to agree on which categories different points belong in. PMI does not involve analysis or assessment – what one person sees as a plus someone else may see as a minus.

For example, if you propose to move a team to a new open plan environment, a plus for one person may be the increased opportunity for social networking but this may be a minus for someone else. You can adapt this exercise to use individually, or with your project team, or with your stakeholders. There are no right and wrong answers – it simply aids your perception and understanding of a given idea, proposal or plan. It can be useful to conduct at an individual level before moving on to a team level so that you can clearly differentiate between your own perception and that of team members. It can also be useful in understanding differences within the team, thereby identifying potential for conflict, providing an opportunity to manage this at an early stage.

The third dimension to the exercise – the Interesting points – can contribute to creativity and innovation within the project and identify issues that may spark further development if they cannot be addressed within the current project. Returning to our example of moving to an open plan environment it may be of interest to see if a sense of community develops or if the group develops a system for 'policing' noise.

Our personal point of view and perspective is important, but it is essential to know when it is just our own view rather than one that is shared by others. In busy times it is easy to make an assumption that our view is commonly held or popular, but we need to check this out and not be surprised if others see the situation differently. It is also useful to reflect on the unintended consequences that changes bring about and try to make these positive experiences for the team. The 'On the Spot' exercise in Box 6.2 is an opportunity to recognize your own perspective of a change in your work environment, and to compare it with the perspective of a colleague.

Box 6.2

'On the Spot' – Recognizing your own perspective

1. Identify a small-scale change that will impact on you at work shortly – for example a new manager arriving, a new policy being implemented, or an aspect of your service discontinuing.

2. Write down the pluses, minuses and points of interest from your perspective. Remember you are looking at what the change means to you, not what you think others will think about it.

3. You might find the 'points of interest' quite difficult to identify. Spend some time thinking about the unanswered questions the proposed change highlights – it is from these that the points of interest are most likely to emerge.

4. Reflect on your response and consider whether others might have answered differently.

If you have a trusted colleague who is also going to be affected by the change ask them to do the same exercise and then discuss your answers together, taking note of the similarities and differences.

Chapter summary

In this chapter we have focused particularly on the 'people management' aspects of your project. By now you will be able to differentiate between different groups of project stakeholders and engage each group effectively, taking account of the level of involvement needed for the project to be successful. You will also have reflected on the differences between managing a project team and an operational team and may have needed to adapt your management style and approach in order to get the best out of them. Finally you will have considered your current network and whether you need to expand your contacts or be more proactive in maintaining the ones you already have.

In Chapter 7 we will consider how to deliver your project by managing risk and change effectively.

Action checklist

- Make sure you know who your stakeholders are and determine the most effective means of engaging them throughout the project life cycle.

- Note your own approach to managing uncertainty and adapt this to the needs of the project.

- Review your approach to supervision and whether this is the most appropriate for team work.

- Review your team management style and adapt to a coaching style if appropriate.

- Be proactive in developing contacts and networks that will assist you in your role as project manager.

Chapter 7

Delivering Your Project

Introduction

As we noted in Chapter 1, the social care sector is vulnerable to periods of austerity and renewal, and social work and social care managers need to be able to maintain the quality of services through times of political and economic fluctuation. So it is absolutely vital that project managers are able to assess and manage the risks involved. In this chapter we will consider how we assess risk, what elements of a project are likely to increase risk, individual perception of risk and how this might impact on a project, the significance of decision-making as a key skill in managing risk, and the tools that can be used to assist the process. We will look at how to identify risk factors and to map and analyse project risks as well as thinking about prevention of risk and the use of projects to promote service improvements.

What do we mean by 'risk'?

In social work, risk management is commonplace. Working with vulnerable people requires a keen surveillance of risk to health and wellbeing so we have an understanding of the complexity and significance of risk assessment, and in project management it is much the same. Risk management is one of the key roles for the social work profession as defined by Skills for Care (2002), with a requirement to be able to facilitate safe and professional working practices, and the Department of Health (2007a) and the Social Care Institute for Excellence (2005) have issued guidance to inform practice in this area. There are a number of factors which need to be considered, some of which can be assessed with some degree of objectivity and others which will be more subjective. We will begin by considering the more objective factors.

How do we assess it?

Assessment of risk is the consideration of a number of variables:

- the probability of something happening

- the potential impact if it happens

- the timing of its occurrence.

This is an assessment that we make regularly in our lives. For example, you have a monthly supervision session booked in your diary for later in the day but there is a crisis emerging with a service user which you may need to become involved in. So, you assess the probability of you having to become involved and the potential impact, that is, the disruption that this may cause to your supervision and the timing – is it possible you will resolve the service user's problem before the supervision session or can your involvement be delayed until after it?

In order to make the assessment in the first place, though, you were given a prompt – someone told you a problem was emerging. In other words there was an indicator that alerted you to the need to carry out the assessment. In social work it is service users' vulnerability that acts as a key indicator, and change in their lives that acts as a trigger to increased risk. But what are the indicators in project management – how will you know if the probability of an untoward event is increasing?

There are a number of factors that are risk indicators, and while this is not an exhaustive list, keeping a watchful eye on each of these will aid the assessment and management of risk:

- *Experience level of those involved in the project.* We have already acknowledged in previous chapters that each project is unique and so everyone involved will feel some degree of inexperience, but learning needs to be used from previous project development. One of the benefits of experience is that we become less perturbed when something unexpected happens. It can be like driving a car. If you talk to some inexperienced car drivers they will say that they plan their route carefully, avoiding situations that they might find hazardous until their confidence increases. If they encounter an unforeseen danger during this phase they may panic or become indecisive. Once their confidence increases they are unperturbed by any eventuality and will drive through areas unknown to them assuredly. So it is with project management – the route may be unfamiliar but the participants have the confidence, developed through experience, to navigate a successful way through. This is illustrated very clearly by Colin, who took on more and more responsibility as a service user as his experience developed and his confidence along with it.

- *Source of funding/amount of money involved.* Clearly, projects involving larger sums of money have more to lose than those with smaller amounts and the penalties for not delivering on time are likely to be greater. It is also important to think about where the money is being sourced and whether there are potential risks involved, for example the possibility of funding being withdrawn or the funding organization defaulting before completion of the project. This is particularly evident in Claire's account. When the funding for dementia services was reduced she observed that 'relationships [were] falling apart as leaders retreat[ed] into their silo management, partly due to a need to protect their own finances'.

- *Technology.* In spite of colossal developments over the last two decades, the stability of the technological environment is still questionable and variable. Some large projects, such as the computerization of the NHS patient records, have proved to be costly failures and it is unlikely that any project will be free of technological input. We all enjoy the benefits of technology when it works for us but curse its limitations when it does not, so particular care needs to be taken in determining the degree to which project success is dependent on technological performance.

- *Project complexity.* By their nature projects are complex, but some are even more so than others. These tend to be the ones that involve multiples – for example, multiple locations, multiple sources of funding, multiple stakeholders. The greater the complexity, the greater the chance of conflict, error and misunderstanding.

- *Vulnerability of service users.* Increased vulnerability means that there are fewer alternative sources of support for people. Lorraine's and Deborah's case studies illustrate project management being used effectively in challenging situations to protect very vulnerable people. Vulnerability may well make success less easily achievable and also increases the potential impact of failure.

- *Stakeholder support and expectations.* Organizational management support is included in this factor. As we saw in Fiona's case study, organizational support can ease the way for working differently. Where this is more tenuous there is an increased chance of the project being terminated along its journey. One of the influences on this will be other stakeholder expectations. If these challenge the organization's way of operating or threaten its credibility the project will become increasingly vulnerable.

The National Programme for IT in the NHS combines all of these factors and illustrates the potential for risks to increase and chances of success to decrease as the project progresses. The National Audit Office's interim report on the patient record system development stated that:

> progress against plans has fallen far below expectations and the Department has not delivered care records systems across the NHS, or with anywhere near the completeness of functionality that will enable it to achieve the original aspirations of the Programme... We conclude that the £2.7 billion spent on care records systems so far does not represent value for money, and we do not find grounds for confidence that the remaining planned spend of £4.3 billion will be different. (NAO 2011a, p.13)

These are particular factors which you, as the project manager, will need to take account of; however, by their very nature, projects incur increased risk. The combination of uniqueness, innovation and pressure to complete on time and within budget inevitably increase the level of susceptibility to risk so, although there may be a degree of fluctuation, risk will be a fairly constant companion throughout your project journey.

As you consider the list of factors above, it may strike you that, although there are inherent risks in many things we do in life, a significant amount of risk is of our own creation. With the exception of the vulnerability of service users, we contribute to a greater or lesser degree to the level of risk that exists within the project. We have opportunities to influence or control the experience of the team, the project funding, the use of technology, the complexity of the project and the expectations of stakeholders, but maybe not to the extent we would like. As our level of influence increases, so does our ability to assess and manage the risks, but what this really means in practice is that we will be more involved in and responsible for the decision-making associated with the project.

Decision-making skills

Skilled decision-making is vital to the success of the project. It has been argued that this is one of the most significant factors in determining the success or failure of a project (Meier 2008) and it is essentially the initial decisions which are crucial, creating 'quality at entry' (Williams and Samset 2010, p.39). Yet it may be that 40–50 per cent of the decisions managers make turn out to be incorrect (Pedler, Burgoyne and Boydell 2007). We all make decisions every day and may consider ourselves quite proficient, but we may not always be aware of the accuracy of our decision-making.

Avoiding reactive decision-making

To develop our decision-making skills we need to understand how we prefer or tend to make decisions and we also need to be able to see a wider perspective – similar to playing chess we need an awareness of the implications of our decisions. It is also critical that we recognize the negativity of the word 'risk' and our own perception of this. When we talk about risk we are referring to issues that are uncertain and there is an element of chance regarding their outcome. But chance is quite positive – no-one worries about the risk of winning the lottery; we hope we have a chance of winning it and yet the degree of uncertainty associated with risk and chance is the same. However, in a culture of blame we focus on managing risk rather than managing uncertainty, and yet we should be steering our project to success rather than it happening by chance in just the same way that we need to be steering it away from danger.

If we focus too much on managing the negative possibilities rather than all uncertainty we will develop an approach to management which is aimed at avoidance of the bad (reactive, controlling, restrictive), rather than adopting an approach which enables the good (proactive, experimental, innovative). We need to achieve a balance, but our ability to do this will be influenced by our personal perception of uncertainty. Some of us will naturally veer towards the more cautious approach while others will be more speculative. Both will be able to justify their approach in relation to the dangers or opportunities it addresses, so how do we achieve a balance?

Rational or intuitive decision-making?

Pedler *et al.* (2007) suggest that there are two different approaches to making decisions – a rational approach based on planning and analysis and an intuitive approach based on 'hunches'. This has similarities with de Bono's (1987) Thinking Hats which suggest six approaches to situations:

- creative

- emotional/intuitive

- positive

- critical

- analytical

- strategic.

The suggestion from de Bono and from Pedler *et al.* is that we need to use all perspectives in order to determine the most appropriate decisions. The starting point has to be recognition of our own preferred approach and, although we will use a combination, by reflecting on the decisions we have made we can identify the main influences. From that we can determine our development needs and strategies for ensuring a holistic approach to decision-making which may include identifying colleagues to provide certain other perspectives.

The 'On the Spot' activity in Box 7.1 provides an opportunity for you to assess making decisions.

Just enough information?

There is also a suggestion that, while some decisions need to take account of as much associated information as possible, in other circumstances this can be a hindrance. Although Williams and Samset (2010) acknowledge that inadequate information has been the cause of some bad decision-making in project management, they also argue that in the initial stages when information may be limited this can be a benefit, helping the manager to focus and retain flexibility.

Outcome evaluation focus

From the very beginning the manager needs to focus on outcome evaluation. Determining achievable, meaningful and transparent goals has challenged health and social work services for decades. The subjectivity of quality of life changes can easily result in agreeing goals which are measurable but do not reflect the essence of the intended outcome. We can spend many frustrating hours trying to find the right words to express the outcome we want to achieve. We may never identify the perfect combination of words but by addressing four key issues we will ensure that the outcome encompasses our intent (Dartington-I 2006, p.2):

- What is being addressed (i.e. the purpose of the project).
- Who will benefit.
- The direction of change.
- The degree of change and the time period (this will help to identify quality and resource issues).

Once you have established agreement to these questions, planning the project from inception to evaluation becomes more manageable.

Box 7.1

'On the Spot' – Making decisions

Consider some of the major decisions you have made in your work and personal life. These might include, for example, applying for a job, buying a house, reorganizing the workplace and making savings.

You probably used a combination of some or all of de Bono's six approaches: creative; emotional/intuitive; positive; critical; analytical; and strategic.

Which approach do you think was the most dominant in helping you to make a decision in each situation?

Communicating decisions

Once decisions have been made, determining how to disseminate the relevant information is key to their successful implementation. Lorraine's case study illustrates how to communicate clearly and effectively with all involved parties during an investigation of suspected adult abuse. Her work provides a template for local authorities to project manage incidences of suspected abuse in residential care, and there are a number of features which are emphasized:

- *Clarity of roles and responsibilities.* A job title is often insufficient to describe what somebody is responsible for. You will note in Lorraine's case study that some of the roles are established purely for the duration of the investigation, such as work managers and document controllers. Although there are strong clues in the titles, the specifics of these roles are spelt out to avoid any possible gaps and overlaps.

- *Clarity of stages.* The template explains the various points at which the investigation might terminate and under what circumstances it will continue to the next stage.

- *Strategy development.* There are specific strategies addressing quality, risk and communications which are aimed at safeguarding residents, processing information well and achieving measured outcomes. Through these three strategies some of the major causes of project failure are overtly addressed. They pre-empt difficulties which might otherwise appear and ensure proactive project management.

Depending on the nature of the project there might be other strategies developed, for example IT or finance management, neither of which is significantly influential in this particular project.

The transparency and clarity in Lorraine's case study contrast starkly with the interim conclusions of the National Audit Office in respect of the National Programme for IT (NAO 2011a). Uncertainty and lack of clarity relating to future budgets, future costs, transfer costs, future management arrangements and future liability are all highlighted as risk factors in the report which recommends that the business case needs to be revisited.

A project which spans more than a decade is bound to encounter change along the way, so the importance of the decision-making and clarity of information becomes even more important. We are told that hindsight is a wonderful thing, but in project management it really is not worth very much. What we have to demonstrate is foresight, which a template such as Lorraine's enables us to do, and the ability to respond to changing circumstances along the way.

Assessing risk probability and impact

You will recall that at the beginning of the chapter we highlighted three important considerations in risk management: probability, impact and timing. We cannot address every single risk factor relating to a project, so having identified the potential risk factors we need to be able to differentiate between them so that we can manage them.

One tool for analysis is the Risk Rating Matrix, based on the process recommended by Standards Australia and Standards New Zealand (2004). This model suggests four stages:

- Decide the context for risk.
- Identify risks.
- Begin analysis.
- Risk Rating Matrix.

The first of these is a factor which we have not yet considered – the context of risk. Although we have looked at how our individual perceptions of risk vary, we have assumed so far that our perceptions of the impact of risk are shared, but this is unlikely. Put simply, if you have £5 and lose it, and your friend has £50 and also loses £5, the impact of the loss on each of you will be different because the context in which you experienced the loss is different. So it is with project risks. The most significant difference is likely to be that between the impact on the organization (or sponsor of the project) and the impact on the service users, so setting your risk analysis in context is critical.

In Chapter 4 Colin shared his experience of becoming involved in a training and employment project. Because he had a background in IT, problems relating to technology began to be referred to him and the trainer without considering the context. Colin had previously experienced mental ill health and had become involved in the project as a service user, but initially there was a lack of consideration shown about this which he recalls had a detrimental effect on his health.

Having identified the risks, the analysis is based on risk probability and risk impact. The probability can be assessed numerically, for example a 1 in 10 chance through to a 1 in a million chance, or on a scale from 'unlikely to ever happen' through to 'highly probable'. Suggested categories for assessment are:

- *Personal impact.* This might be the impact on service users or an individual member of the team, or the sponsoring organization, for example. In Lorraine's case study there is the potential for physical harm to come to residents, while in Deborah's there is risk of service closure, so the personal risks are very high and the triggers need to be clearly identified.

- *Quality impact.* The degree to which it will affect the achievement of the agreed standard.

- *Financial impact.* Budget losses or additional costs incurred as a consequence.

- *Public confidence/reputation.* This can range from there being no public interest through to an incident resulting in a public inquiry.

- *Complaint or claim.* This includes criminal and civil action.

The 'On the Spot' activity in Box 7.2 is an example of a risk mapping analysis. By making the risk visible it becomes more manageable – when we think about risks they can seem overwhelming and become immobilizing, but writing them down enables us to begin to take control. We can share our concerns as necessary, clearly illustrating our analysis to those who need to know. We can differentiate between and prioritize risks through this process.

Box 7.2

'On the Spot' – Risk mapping analysis

1. Identify a project you are currently working on – this may be a specific, time-limited piece of work, such as an investigation or a new development, for example.

2. Identify the risks involved – you might find it helpful to use the headings of service users, stakeholders (including organizational management), staff experience, finding source, technology and project complexity, but add others as appropriate.

3. Assess the probability of each risk.

4. Assess the potential impact of each risk using the headings: personal impact, quality impact, financial impact, public confidence/reputation and complaint or claim.

5. Identify immediate action for those risks with high probability and high impact.

6. Identify preventive measures for those risks with medium–high probability but low impact assessment.

7. Identify preventive measures and contingency plans for those with medium–high impact assessment but low probability.

8. Consider the remaining risks – can these be managed as they occur? If not, then develop an action plan.

Managing change

Managing innovative people

As we saw in Chapter 3, project management requires the ability to be able to introduce and manage change at times while being undeviating at others, and an element of the skill is in being able to distinguish when each is needed. Some people are more averse to change than others, and Rogers (1995) argues that we range from those who seek out new ways of working irrespective of whether they may be needed (innovators) through to those who avoid change until it is forced upon them (laggards). Most of us fall somewhere in between and will move between being early or late adopters depending on our situation at the time. However, those who are attracted to project management or project team work are more likely to be towards the early adopter–innovator end of the spectrum as change is inevitable. So it is more likely that as the project manager you will need to put more energy into keeping the team on track, preventing them from introducing yet more new ideas and extending the project beyond its parameters, than into urging them to try the unfamiliar.

Responding to a problem or an opportunity?

It is important that you assess why the change is needed and how best to determine the way forward. One question to ask yourself is whether it is a response to a problem or an opportunity. For example, if you are making a cake and drop all the eggs on the floor, then your response will be different from if you are making a cake and decide towards the end that it would be better with icing and cherries on the top. In the first situation change of some nature is essential as you have a problem and cannot continue with the original plan, whereas in the second your original plan is fine but you are tempted to change it to improve the quality. This is relevant to Deborah's case study. Although Deborah's project is a response to a problem (the need to reduce the budget by 15 per cent), the initial proposal – to develop a community scheme, recruiting volunteers to provide some of the support to service users – can be viewed as an opportunity.

We need to remember that opportunities have an impact and a cost too. Adding icing and cherries might blow your budget, or it might no longer meet your stakeholders' requirements as quality is subjective, or you might not complete your task on time. Although Deborah's community scheme proposal has the potential to make the required savings, it also has the potential to significantly alter the way in which the team provides services. This may have a greater impact than simply reducing the level of service delivery through existing methods of working. So any potential or possible changes need to be questioned, even if they appear to be positive.

Systems approach to change

A good rule of thumb is to use a systems approach to change. This demonstrates the links between various aspects of an organization or project, arguing that a change in one will have an impact on the others. There are different ways of categorizing the sub-systems of the project, but a useful one, proposed by the Open University (2004), is:

- vision/mission
- leadership; strategy

- skills

- technology

- communication

- structure.

By thinking about each of the sub-systems it is possible to consider the potential impact that a change within one of them will have on the others. The suggestion is that changes should emanate from the vision/mission, leadership or technological sub-systems. The other sub-systems need to be considered in terms of the likely impact, but the change should not be initiated there. This is helpful in deciding whether a change should happen or not as we can identify its origins and question whether it is an appropriate response.

It is important to note that the conclusion of the National Audit Office in the interim report on the National Programme for IT in the NHS is to recommend that the business case is revisited: 'there is a compelling case for the recently announced Whitehall-wide review to re-evaluate the business case for the Programme to determine what should happen now to safeguard against further loss of public value' (NAO 2011a, p.14). In a systems approach this equates to going back to the vision or mission of the project; this will ensure that any proposed changes are linked directly to the intended outcomes, which may need to be amended in light of experience of the project so far.

Balancing business needs and creativity

Although this systems model does not specify funding sources or budgets as one of the sub-systems, it does recognize the significance of culture in influencing all of the sub-systems. Increasingly in social work we operate in a business environment and certainly in project management this is essential. Developing a working environment that recognizes the business needs and the need for innovation and creativity is quite a challenge, but one approach that enables projects or organizations to recognize both is appreciative inquiry, described as 'the co-operative co-evolutionary search for the best in people, their organizations, and the world around them' (Cooperrider, Whitney and Stavros 2005, p.3).

Appreciative inquiry fundamentally highlights the difference between seeing a glass as half empty or half full and is founded on the idea that we need to see the glass as half full if we are to manage change effectively. Sometimes when we look at a situation we see the problems, the things that are not working very well, because those are the easiest things to see. It is always easier to spot a mistake than it is to identify what is right. Appreciative inquiry is about focusing on the positives. It is encouraging rather than blaming, an optimistic rather than a pessimistic approach. It encourages us to identify the strengths of the project and identify a means of building on those for service improvement. It involves everyone and is a very proactive means of working with the team and stakeholders, developing a culture which focuses on achieving.

As a project manager you cannot ignore the risks, the problems and the challenges that are an intrinsic part of project management, and much of this chapter has focused on those. However, they can be debilitating and immobilizing if you are working within a culture that is fearful, timid or disapproving, so it is vital to develop a working environment from the beginning of your project that is sufficiently bold, robust, assertive and critical to address the problems and achieve success.

Chapter summary

There is an element of risk in nearly all that we do, and in order to bring your project to a successful outcome you need to be able to manage the risks effectively. This means being able to recognize the risks, assess their severity and significance and make cohesive and coherent decisions to determine your response to them. Most of us make decisions from a limited perspective, our preferred way of viewing the world, but to ensure our decision-making is a balanced and well-founded response to the situation we need to consider perspectives other than our preferred one. In this chapter we have looked at a process for doing that. We have also highlighted the importance of adopting a positive approach to change management which seeks to build on existing strengths and of recognizing the links between different parts of a project which mean that change in one part will also result in change in other parts.

In Chapter 8 we will move on to considering the final part of the project process – closure and evaluation.

Action checklist

- Monitor the risk indicators within your project.
- Develop a risk strategy in response to a risk analysis.

- Check that your decision-making is comprehensive and coherent.

- Ensure that any proposed changes relate to the achievement of the project outcomes.

- Develop an inclusive, questioning and positive working environment in your project.

Chapter 8

Ending Your Project

Introduction

This penultimate chapter explores the importance and contribution of governance to project management and the importance of ending projects properly. Accountability structures and documentation can at times feel like hindering the progress of trying to ensure good services to people who need them. This chapter will reflect on the importance of governance and develop skills to deliver the project, highlighting the structured way that it enables the project to be controlled and well ordered through using tools such as reporting, risk assessment and reporting. Whilst this might feel bureaucratic, accountability is a core value in the social work and social care sector. This has been highlighted by the proposed Standards for Employers and Supervision Framework produced by the Social Work Reform Board (2011).

Governance was a key element of Public Administration (Hood 1991) and emphasized the importance of legislation, rules, guidelines and the role of bureaucracy in developing and implementing policy. The rise of New Public Management and its emphasis on learning lessons from the private sector; greater emphasis on the use of managers rather than professional discretion; control; evaluation; performance management; and audit (Hafford-Letchfield 2007) has had a profound impact on accountability. A critique of these changes is beyond the remit of this book, but the impact of this change resonates in project management tools and methods – that is, project governance. Project governance will be discussed in more detail in the next section of this chapter.

In this chapter, we will be focusing on the ending of the project, whether this is because the project has come to its natural end, for example where the project is complete, or as a result of the project ending earlier than planned for other reasons such as changes to legislative requirements that cannot be accommodated in the project, non-delivery, or occurrence of a major risk such as discussed in Chapter 7. It is important that the end of all projects is recognized, success celebrated and lessons learnt rather than having the project seeming to fall off the end of a cliff into obscurity. We have all experienced tasks to which we have given a lot of time and commitment as well as making many personal sacrifices. This will be the same for people who are participating in projects. In social work and social care, despite being people-focused, we can sometimes forget to fully acknowledge all the effort and commitment made by teams and stakeholders during projects, particularly when we are exhausted and often grateful for the end of a difficult project. In this chapter we are going to identify the importance of governance within a project and how this cultivates robust arrangements for any projects that you may lead. We will also look at the skills involved in developing and planning the end of a project.

Project governance

Project governance is a term used to describe those support and accountability processes that are put in place by the organization to sustain successful delivery of the project. This governance support would comprise structures, systems, processes and roles that are critical in ensuring that the project remains focused and deliverable. For instance this could include the need for regular project reporting of a social care project to the Social Services Committee in a local authority by the project sponsor and project manager.

Throughout this chapter we will be using a case study involving a new older people's 40-bed semi-independent and residential facility and corresponding changes to community services to illustrate many of the arguments made. The facility was being developed in collaboration with the local authority and the NHS, with the charity taking responsibility for the new build and the local authority (LA) leading on the service changes. An independent project manager was appointed, with staff seconded to the project team from the LA, NHS and the charity.

Before being able to commit to investing £12 million in the new build, the charity needed to:

- ensure that they had secured long-term commissioner funding

- secure agreement that local authority social work and NHS community teams wanted to change referral and community support services

- obtain a guarantee that the local housing authority wanted eligible existing tenants in poor housing to be offered supportive accommodation within the new development.

Corporate governance comprises a range of relationship, reporting and accountability structures through which the organization evaluates whether its objectives, quality and ethical standards are being met and includes ways in which monitoring is undertaken. By way of example in the social care sector, this could include board reports, reports to elected officials and stakeholders (including users of services), as well as regular management reports. The relationship between the project sponsor (discussed in Chapters 1, 3 and 4), the project manager, stakeholders and the organization's management structure is important. You will recall that we have previously emphasized the importance that projects in social care and social work meet the needs of all stakeholders, which ensures that all stakeholders are committed to the success of the project. A project's 'risk profile' can increase if all stakeholders are not committed to its success, as we discussed in Chapter 7. This requires that the project team ensures that parts of the project are not prioritized above others to give preference to certain stakeholder needs. For instance, prioritizing the financial savings of a social care project and neglecting the importance of service users and professional needs.

As a result, the key purpose in establishing governance structures is to ensure the following:

- The project has clear objectives. You will recall from Chapter 3 that this is undertaken before the project starts, but with the appropriate approval provided by the relevant accountable body. This structure will vary depending on the agency or department, but could include the board in an independent sector organization, or social services committee in a local authority.

- The project has clarity in how it will meet those objectives.

- The project has a clear and transparent way of measuring progress of the project in achieving those agreed objectives.

It is important also to take a critical view of projects and to recognize that there may be a temptation to be more optimistic about the potential benefits of a project, to deflate the risks or potential costs or not to collect appropriate performance data (NAO 2011b). The lack of healthy accountability and governance arrangements may encourage over-optimistic projections and underlines the need for robust accountability processes. The project sponsor is normally the individual who would need to account for any discrepancy between project projections and its implementation outcome at the end, but the project manager should be mindful of these potential risks.

Project relationships

The relationships both within the project team and between the project manager and project sponsor are critical for successful projects. The project sponsor and the project manager, in particular, have an important relationship and are required to work closely together. It is normally the project sponsor who will clarify the parameters within which the project manager will work. You will recall that in Chapter 1 we explored the advantages of the project manager being able to work outside of traditional line management structures, and to do so effectively they will require clarity from the project sponsor.

The project sponsor needs to be able to trust the project manager, as the project manager will be required to make day-to-day decisions without constant recourse to the project sponsor. In order to do this the project manager needs to have the project sponsor and project board's confidence and agreement. Ways in which the project manager could assure this may include:

- providing qualitative and quantitative information, such as reports on progress, actions being taken in response to risks, etc., to demonstrate that the project will be successful and achieve its goals

- providing assurance that the correct processes are in place to ensure project delivery

- demonstrating that the project will be delivered to the agreed budget, quality and performance targets and timescales

- through transparency exhibiting the reliability, honesty and effectiveness of the project manager

- guaranteeing that there are sufficient procedures and controls in place to ensure the above.

The 'On the Spot' activity in Box 8.1 is an exercise in evaluating whether a project is fit for purpose, and whether the project manager is sufficiently in control.

Box 8.1

'On the Spot' – Fit for purpose?

Consider a project that you are familiar with or one of the projects discussed in Chapter 2 and weigh up the following:

1. Will the project be fit for purpose and perform to achieve the required outcomes?

2. Has the right process been adopted to deliver the project, given any constraints on timescale, budget and resourcing?

3. Does the project manager have this project under control? Are they being honest about progress, risks and other issues that may cause problems?

In Fiona's case study, it would be advisable to develop a robust business case and project plan which provides sufficient assurance and evidence that the proposed project will meet the agreed project requirements. Regular written updates and verbal presentations on progress would further add demonstrable credibility to progress. The stakeholder project agreement and regular reporting of progress to both stakeholders and a project management governance committee would highlight ongoing pressures, concerns, performance and remedial actions being undertaken, should the project not be achieving its milestones or its objectives. Reports would normally include outcomes against objectives, milestones, budgets and an update on the risks to completion. This clear, transparent and regular written reporting would update on problems, agreed changes to the project, risks and actions being taken to mitigate these. The publication of regular project meeting minutes, including those between the project sponsor and project board, facilitates transparency and accountability. In respect of the frequency of reporting, verbal reports to the project sponsor would be undertaken once a week and report on risks, outstanding issues and actions being taken. Written reports should be made every two weeks and would contain performance data, costs, performance against timescales and risks.

The role of a project office

If you are undertaking a large-scale project, it may be supported by a 'project office', which includes infrastructure such as project and finance administration, specialist staff and the project manager. Duggal (2007) identifies the project office's role as normally to:

- support the planning and control of the large project

- support the development of policies, procedures and systems and also support the development of reports

- manage data on progress and provide additional support as necessary to aspects of the project

- support communication and manage relationships.

In considering our chapter example: for the housing authority, a number of their properties were considered unsuitable for the current tenants. The project involved significant negotiation and planning just to get the facility design agreed by the stakeholders, who included the local authority, social service department, local housing trust, the NHS, older people's charities, service users and professionals. Once construction of this multi-million-pound facility commenced, the project office was involved in not only managing the new build, but also supporting changes to local referral policies, supporting transition for residents, and managing the anxieties of the local residents, services, professionals and the charity that also needed to recruit staff and fully equip the service. The project manager was therefore managing a large multi-agency project by needing to manage both construction and service redesign.

Some of the day-to-day tasks that the project team was therefore involved in included:

- Maintaining and managing the master project plan – this would involve agreeing changes to the project plan and making adjustments as a result of these agreements. In the example of the new development, the project office had to amend the project plan and its roll-out when building permission was withheld, temporarily, on discovery of newts on the building site. Building permission in this circumstance was withheld for three months to enable their breeding to be unimpaired. This required substantial project rescheduling and additional cost.

- Managing the resource plan (schedule of what will be required and when, to ensure that resources are in place when they are needed) in large projects, such as in the older people's service example, may actually involve a number of smaller projects under the overall project umbrella. For instance, the change in resources had implications for the local social work and primary care teams, in that it widened the opportunity and resources available for local older people in need of support. This had a knock-on impact to referral and community support work patterns.

- Supporting control of the project – by providing administrative support, that is, setting up and supporting meetings and keeping detailed financial records, project managers for various sub-processes could focus on managing the project. As a result, the project office would review the consequences of decisions made, undertake 'what if' analysis to support decision-making, revise plans and develop 'work to do' lists.

- Progress reporting for all stakeholders and managing the relationships with all stakeholders, including helping to manage anxiety and additional queries.

- Maintaining document control. All projects require documentation, including invoicing etc., meeting minutes, correspondence, written agreements and variations, all of which need to be maintained, logged and stored securely. It is important to ensure that proper sign-off of project stages, together with quality control, is undertaken and subcontractor information is managed. Each of the project stages links directly to the tasks, tools and themes we have discussed in Chapters 3, 4 and 7 such as risk management and stakeholder involvement.

Project governance therefore is a process which is undertaken throughout the life of a project, from its early beginnings to its closure.

Project closure

Project closure is the end-point of all projects. The reasons for closure can be as a result of the project being completed, mutual agreement or the project being ended early. An example of a high-profile project failure is that of the National Offender Management Service (NOMS) implementation of a new IT system to manage offenders across the probation and prison service by January 2008. The National Audit Office (2009) highlighted that, despite the project-agreed cost of £234 million over its lifetime from 2004 to 2015, by 2007 the project was already two years behind schedule, £155 million had already been spent and the projected lifetime cost was £690 million. As in this example, not all failed projects are terminated, but projects can be ended early if they may be considered no longer viable, their risk profile changes or the project is not delivering on its key success factors. Examples therefore in the social care sector might include the withdrawal of funding, or unintended consequences where changes to referral systems are resulting in harm or delay in responses to service users.

The ending of projects in social care and social work should ensure that the project is closed down:

- in a structured and organized way

- so that all aspects of the project are properly accounted for and handed over in a well-thought-out and controlled way.

Unless the project is closed in this way, the recriminations and blaming about its failure will start, and at its extreme this can involve threatened legal action where excess costs have been incurred. By ensuring that you have full stakeholder engagement throughout the project, these risks can be reduced significantly, as well as being able to manage stakeholder expectations as part of an ongoing process, as we explored in Chapter 6. Since all projects end, it is good practice for the ending to be discussed and planned for at the start of the project. Examples of this planning could include who will be responsible for the new facility or process at the end of the project and how transfer of ownership of the facility or process will take place. Finally, the termination of the project enables acknowledgement of contributions, closure of financial accounts, and transfer of legal ownership and written acceptance of transfer. Lorraine's case study in Chapter 2 and Claire's experience in Chapter 4 provide good examples of this.

Important steps in closure

Stakeholders being impressed by the skills of the project team and the overall success of the project is important in ensuring that the change starts with a positive expectation. In doing this it is necessary for the following to be undertaken:

- Ensure that the client has accepted the project. This would include a walkthrough of the final completion and the client verifying in writing that they accept the project deliverable.

- Complete all the steps necessary to pass over responsibility for the completed project.

- Ensure that all contractual and financial obligations have ended, for example temporary staff and contractors have been paid and any performance reviews of staff are completed.

- Review lessons to be learnt, both positive and negative.

- Update and close the final project management documentation.

- Publicize and celebrate the project's success.

In our example of the new older people's residential facility, project closure was undertaken through:

- a variety of structured meetings involving all stakeholders for all aspects of the project, that is, construction, referrals, housing

- open days where stakeholders were invited to tour the facility, meet key stakeholders and view the agreed project outcomes

- the sign-off of a formal project acceptance by the charitable trust in which they accepted responsibility for the new building

- formal acceptance by each of the statutory and non-statutory organizations of the project

- official stakeholder meetings to review the project and its outcomes

- press releases to highlight the completion of the project and acknowledge the contributions of all involved.

Problems in closing projects

Closing a project may not always be as simple as we would hope or as suggested in the example given in this chapter, and frequent challenges are experienced:

- The lack of time between projects for reflection and recovery between projects. Due to the need for efficiency, experienced project managers may be asked to start a new project before the old one ends. This, whilst possibly being perceived as efficient at one level, may also increase the risks of poor closure on the existing project.

- Failing to pass accountability on completion to the client. In the rush and euphoria of a successful project, there can be errors or slippage in the transfer of responsibility of the project, or facilities, to the new owners. Whilst the organization might be happy with the success of the project, the failure to transfer the ongoing maintenance and processes involved in the new process or building can result in later failure or recriminations. For instance, failing to transfer responsibility for equipment in the new residential facility to the charity responsible for maintenance may result in equipment failure, additional risks to service users and poor service delivery. Whilst this didn't happen in the example, failure to hand over responsibility for hoists, for instance, could result in difficulties later.

- The culture of the organization may not value the importance of project closure and evaluation. If this is the case it might make it very difficult for the project manager and project team to undertake these activities. It is therefore often better to plan and agree for this to be undertaken at the start of the project when everyone is enthusiastic.

- Honest review of lessons learnt. It is tempting to celebrate the success of a project. Often this will require 'political' support and courage from the project sponsor and project board to ensure that the organization recognizes and enacts the learning.

The 'On the Spot' activity in Box 8.2 provides an opportunity for you to think about project closure, using the case studies of Chapter 2 and the user experiences of Chapter 4, and reflecting on the skills that you have developed through reading this book. Ideas that you may consider would probably include:

- To successfully conclude a project, it is important that previous stages in the project plan are completed. For instance in Lorraine's case study, the fact-finding stage needed to be adequately resolved in order for that phase to end and enable the project to move to its next stage.

- The involvement of all stakeholders and the client is important for formally accepting transfer and responsibility. The lead agency and the provider have to be committed to ensure that the process is owned and that both organizations can continue to improve services after the project is completed.

- The lessons learnt would apply for all involved and, whilst some of these may be shared, others would require the respective organizations to review and support these. This may have implications for organizational culture, staffing, individual learning and changes to existing governance structures.

- Project members need feedback on areas where they did well, as well as learning points for the future.

Box 8.2

'On the Spot' – Ending your project

In this activity you should reflect on the projects and experiences discussed in Chapters 2 and 4 of this book. Using your own experience and the knowledge acquired from reading the book, consider a social care or social work project you might be involved in:

1. Identify what key steps need to be completed at the end of each stage in a project.

2. How might the project owner formally accept the project and what would this entail?

3. How might lessons be learnt and received by the project team and the organization? Are there any things you could do to maximize their acceptance?

4. What practical arrangement would be made to tie up the resources, finances and people aspects of the project?

5. How might you appraise project members and support them for the future?

Chapter summary

Project management has become a key method of undertaking change within many organizations, including those in social work and social care. In this chapter we have developed a clearer understanding of the nature of governance and how this might help support you in managing projects. It is important that in developing projects you also plan for their ending and consider and incorporate appropriate and robust governance systems to support delivery. Weak governance systems, whilst at one level might seem an easier way forward, may also weaken accountability and transparency. This has implications for the ending of projects. The conclusion is as important as other stages of project delivery, regardless of whether this finishing point is as a result of project completion or early termination. Like many aspects of social work and social care, good endings regardless of difficulty support positive outcomes.

Action checklist

- Reviewing the ending of your project, make certain that the success requirements are clearly identified.

- Clarify and ensure that the governance and accountability systems that are established are 'fit for purpose' and will support project delivery.

Chapter 9

Project Management Across Diverse Cultures

Lambert Engelbrecht

Introduction

Throughout this book we have sought to develop your skills and understanding of project management and have used case studies to help your understanding from a largely UK context. This final chapter seeks to take a wider perspective and to develop a framework of project management across different cultures. This is important in an increasingly globalized world and has implications for the assumptions that we may make as project managers. Indeed, Spolander *et al.* (2011) in their study of Canada, South Africa and England highlighted that the social-political contexts for the delivery of social welfare services vary considerably. Project managers in the social work and social care sector should therefore be mindful of globalization and the migration of people and cultures. Hence, unsubstantiated assumptions cannot be made about cultures in project management as a result. Additionally, project managers who wish to work within other international social welfare contexts as part of their career progression should develop their skills and understanding to reflect this global reality.

Previous chapters have explained the tasks, roles, processes, tools and techniques of project management. Chapter 6 has already recognized the importance of project managers in working with people participating in projects. This final chapter seeks to develop your skills about the diverse contexts in which you will be required to work with people. These cultural contexts determine people's values, including what they believe is right and wrong for them. Project managers who apply their own values as they try to understand project participants' values will certainly create embarrassment and provoke conflict. Consequently, as a project manager, you should appreciate that project participants' values are ingrained in their diverse cultures and carried into their work. Based on this notion, this chapter has been written drawing on the learning you have already developed in delivering projects, but now engaging you to consider a broader context for managing projects. However, due to our sensitivity for the diverse contexts of people's cultural experiences, we are deliberately not seeking to make unsubstantiated assumptions. We will therefore not be offering case studies in this chapter, but will rather focus by means of examples and suggestions on a framework for an understanding of the topic and for the development of skills accordingly.

In this final chapter we are going to examine the implications and need for project management across cultures. This will require being clear about the meaning of diversity and culture and the implications for your project management. We hope that you will be able to recognize cultural dimensions and their impact on project management and be aware of what skills you need to manage projects successfully across cultures.

The need for management across diverse cultures

Changes in life are ongoing as we live in an ever-changing and turbulent world. Much of our uncertainty in the world is the result of globalization, exacerbated by economic forces, technological innovations, government policies and especially the migration of the workforce. Consequently, any work with people, not only internationally but also in local contexts, requires the crossing of cultural borders. One worldview is therefore no longer possible today, and as a result this should be reflected in our thinking about project management. A one-size-fits-all approach or step-by-step quick fix to accommodate different cultures in project management would also be too simplistic (Deresky 2001; Harzing and van Ruysseveldt 2004; Moran, Harris and Moran 2007).

Due to migration between countries the social work and social care workforces have become more diverse. In addition, the recruitment and retention of a highly qualified and competent workforce has become crucial, particularly during periods of recession and austerity, which also results in many organizations merging and/or forming partnerships in projects as well as greater diversification of those working in these systems. As organizations are sub-systems of the larger society, they will include people with a range of societal values, beliefs, ideologies and, above all, diverse cultures. These are ultimately apparent in the attitudes and behaviours of the staff they recruit and the structures created. Cultural diversity not only affects every organization, regardless of size, nature or location, but also managers of projects in these organizations due to changes in decision-making, communication, motivation, negotiation, etc.

Of course, cultural diversity is desirable and not something to be avoided in social work and social care. Our projects may benefit from the diversity of perspectives with less emphasis on conformity to one cultural norm. This can improve creativity; decision-making may potentially account for a wider range of perspectives and lead to a more thorough critical analysis of issues, as we explored in Chapter 3. It is thus essential for successful project management that a project manager should understand how people of different cultures respond in similar situations. These different responses can be translated as cultural dimensions, which suggest ways of reasoning, explaining, perceiving and thinking in different settings.

Diversity and culture

You as a project manager undertake a role in which you go between and within different cultures and as a result must be able to observe, describe and analyse your similarities and differences in order to manage projects successfully. Therefore, a solid understanding of the concepts 'diversity' and 'culture' is essential for any project manager.

Although formulated many decades ago, Gouldner's (1957) conceptualization of 'locals' and 'cosmopolitans' in the workforce is still relevant, especially now in times of globalization and the resulting migration. He proposed that one can determine when a worker is a 'local' or 'cosmopolitan' through inquiring into the individual's object of loyalty, primary reference group and degree of commitment to skills. 'Locals' are defined primarily by their deep-rooted affiliation to specific local communities. In contrast, the affiliation of 'cosmopolitans' to their local community may be loose, and their definition of 'home' may be quite fluid or multi-faceted. The loyalty of 'cosmopolitans' is moreover directed towards their profession and to its values but not necessarily to an organization. Their primary reference group is thus their fellow professionals. 'Local' workers reflect opposite characteristics and, for example, owe loyalty primarily to the organization, and their primary reference group is their immediate supervisor or project manager. They are likely to do what they are told without much questioning, as they want to please their immediate supervisors. They will usually not object if asked to perform a task that is outside their job description and they will pay close attention to rules and procedures. The consequence is that it may be much easier and more beneficial for the project manager to work with 'locals' rather than with 'cosmopolitans', as project managers and 'locals' might share the same values. This 'local–cosmopolitan' relationship may be an oversimplification of the dynamics in project management, but it contributes to our understanding of diversity issues and specifically of cultural diversity.

Past experience suggests that project managers in social work and social care can face complaints by project participants (most likely from 'locals') who perceive cultural differences of other participants as unprofessional behaviour. Project managers' own demographic characteristics and life experiences may also lead to prejudices and stereotyping and can affect their capacity to manage 'cosmopolitans' effectively. Within this context of project management across cultures, prejudice relates to interpersonal hostility directed against project participants, based on their cultural affiliation. In contrast, stereotyping is an over-generalized and a standardized judgement of participants affiliated to a specific culture, and is a denial of their individual differences. Project managers, however, need to be able to recognize the prejudices, stereotypes and behaviours of participants (both 'locals' and 'cosmopolitans') and in themselves that can impinge on their ability to execute their duties. Appreciating the diversity of people's cultures is therefore a prerequisite.

The concept of 'diversity' refers to variation in the qualities of people. The primary dimensions of diversity include inherent differences that cannot be changed and have an impact throughout life. Examples are age, ethnicity, gender, physical abilities, race and sexual orientation. However, the concept 'diversity' is broad and fails to convey what is specifically referred to. The cultural dimension of diversity, therefore, specifically in the context of project management in social work and social care, is exceptionally relevant in a globalized world. This means that you as project manager should always be aware of cultural perspectives. Cultural perspectives are inherent in all people and systems involved in the project and are embedded in all work. As a result it is the lens through which 'others' in the project are viewed and the basis from which interactions with other people should proceed. Indeed, the extent of diverse cultures' influence on project performances is sometimes so profound that it is often unseen. If not understood well and handled proactively, not only will unproductive conflicts result, but potential will go untapped. Although complicated, this means that 'cultural diversity' is rather chameleon-like, with the meaning depending on context and a number of variables, thus colouring one's interpretation of 'culture'.

To define 'culture' as a concept is quite daunting; easy to discuss, distinguish and to identify but difficult to define, as it is an abstract concept holding different meanings for different people in different contexts, and debates on the correct meaning of culture are mostly inconclusive. Kroeber and Kluckhohn (1952) for instance identified more than 200 formal definitions, albeit some time ago, but still there is no single definition. Defining culture within a social work and social care project management context should therefore start with the question of what serves the project manager's needs best in practice.

Various authors on the topic (Hofstede 1980, 2001; Trompenaars and Hampden-Turner 2004) who specifically conceptualize culture within a management context suggest that we may define culture within a framework of:

- patterned ways of thinking, feeling and reacting, acquired and transmitted mainly by symbols, and consisting of traditional ideas and attached values

- the collective programming of the mind that distinguishes the members of one human group from another

- symbols, stories, rituals and a worldview that help people to survive and succeed

- a way in which a group of people solves problems and reconciles dilemmas

- shared motives, values, beliefs, identities and interpretations of significant events resulting from common experiences and transmitted across generations.

These definitions are certainly useful, but have different nuances. It also seems that researchers have adopted particular notions of culture to suit the dominant concerns of the day. However, three categories of aspects of the framework as expounded above are evident in project management:

- visible aspects (e.g. the way project participants speak, dress and eat)

- social aspects (e.g. habits, customs and rituals)

- unconscious aspects (e.g. beliefs, ideas and assumptions that govern the other aspects).

These aspects are shared by members of a culture, learned and/or adopted through membership, and influence the attitudes and behaviours of project participants.

Basically we can define culture in social work and social care project management as the way in which different groups of people do things differently from other groups, and therefore perceive the world differently (Smit and Cronje 1999). Therefore, any project to be managed is the product of the cultural context in which it arises. Consequently, the more we learn about and understand different cultures, the more able we may be to work well across cultures. The 'On the Spot' activity in Box 9.1 invites you to reflect further on culture and contexts in project management.

Box 9.1

'On the Spot' – The impact of culture

Although the important role of culture and contexts in influencing managerial actions is incontestably accepted, several questions emerge as practical implications of culture within the context of project management. Using your skills and the knowledge acquired in this book, reflect on:

1. Where might culture end and personal characteristics begin in a project participant's performance?

2. Might your management style (if it is working well currently) be equally appropriate if used in another culture?

Different cultures often require different approaches by project managers, particularly as organizations and employees do not live in a vacuum and cultural variables are carried into the workplace. In this connection, a number of attempts have been made throughout the past decades to capture the essence of cultural differences and similarities across borders – also referred to as cultural dimensions. An examination of these may help to illuminate the influence of culture on project management.

Cultural dimensions and their impact on project management

The Dutch management researcher Geert Hofstede's model (1980, 2001) of cultural dimensions is probably the most popular and widely disseminated research on culture in relation to management and organizational behaviour. He analysed survey data from a substantial matched-sample, cross-national database and identified four key dimensions of cultural differences, based on the assumption that different cultures can be distinguished by differences in what they value. These differences affect people's perception of work and employee relations and have a detrimental impact on project management.

A fifth dimension to this model was added later, based on research by Bond and associates (Bond and Smith 1996).

Cultural dimensions should not be confused with organizational culture, and in this connection we can convert Hofstede's model of cultural dimensions into the following useful framework with an eye to understand project participants' diverse cultures:

- Culture can develop to involve different aspects of an identity, group or society.

- A society does not have only one culture.

- There are various sub-cultures.

- Culture can be influenced by variables such as class, religion, generations, gender and different regions of a country.

It is important that you note that Hofstede's model of cultural dimensions concerns cultures in different countries rather than individuals and is not absolute, but rather expressed in relative terms. Nevertheless, even such a ground-breaking body of work does not escape criticism and, although not all of Hofstede's ideas may stand up to public scrutiny, the majority of his findings have withstood the times and are still widely used in management across diverse cultures. An excerpt from his model presented here illustrates the need to take this into consideration when managing projects. These core dimensions are expounded as an example of a useful framework in addressing the practical implications of diverse cultures within the context of social work and social care project management. The five core cultural dimensions essentially include the following:

- *Characteristics which revolve around individualism and collectivism.* This dimension is about how people see themselves in relation to others and the extent to which personal freedom and privacy are valued. Individual interests take priority over group interests in individualist cultures. Conversely, people respect and adhere to the norms of the group to which they belong in a collectivist culture.

- *Attitude to power.* Managers operating in a high-power distance culture automatically have higher status than their subordinates, whereas in a low-power distance culture, power and status are not as important as competency and achievement.

- *Tolerance of uncertainty.* This concerns the extent to which people in a culture feel threatened by uncertainty and ambiguity, which in turn determines the number and nature of rules and laws as well as anxiety levels and extent of tolerance of the unpredictable. People from cultures with high uncertainty avoidance will thus resist change and risks, whereas people with low uncertainty avoidance are encouraged to test their ideas and need few rules and regulations to guide them.

- *The dominance of certain values.* This dimension encompasses elements of masculine and feminine oriented values, but entails more than just gender differences. For people in a masculine oriented culture, assertiveness, competition, performance and the acquisition of material objects are important. People from a feminine oriented culture will focus more on quality of life, and show modesty and concern for others.

- *Time orientation.* People from a long-term oriented culture are geared towards the future, value hard work and dedication and have a certain sense of shame. Alternatively, people with a short-term orientation assume that there is an absolute truth, promote the values of the past, show respect for traditions and value social obligations.

Several other significant cultural dimensions may be considered by you, as identified by Kluckhohn and Strodtbeck (1961), Hall and Hall (1990), Schwartz (1992), Trompenaars and Hampden-Turner (2004) and House *et al.* (2004). These dimensions, along which various cultures can be compared, impact for example on projects in terms of people's attitudes towards:

- decision-making
- negotiations
- communication
- relationship with nature and the environment
- interpersonal relationships
- achievements
- approach to work
- rules
- space
- gender.

A more explicit example based on the research of Tayeb (1996), specifically within the English context, is the following:

English people may be inter alia less emotional, less obedient and less friendly than people from some other countries, but are more able to cope with new and uncertain situations, more willing to accept responsibility, more disciplined, more arrogant, more reserved and more individualistic.

These cultural dimensions, as we have already indicated, have specific country connections, which may be transcended to go beyond country borders through groups and individuals all over the world in all spheres of life, modified by the process of acculturation in our contemporary globalized world. Acculturation implies a reciprocal influence of cultures in which cultural dimensions mingle and merge. The examples we presented of cultural dimensions should thus rather be perceived on a continuum, mirroring the extent to which you and project participants relate to specific cultures with distinct dimensions. This continuum of acculturation may entail project participants' and your own movement towards a dominant culture, your ability to live in different worlds, your integration of different cultures, reaffirmation of your traditional culture or even your alienation from all cultures (Berry 1986; Sodowsky and Plake 1992).

These examples emphasize that successful project management practices in one culture may differ from those in another, and that people belonging to different cultures may react differently to certain management styles. It is thus evident that you should possess a range of skills to be able to communicate and collaborate with project participants and systems across diverse cultures.

Skills required by project managers to manage successfully across cultures

Project management across cultures is sometimes perceived as being only about developing awareness and understanding and being non-judgemental rather than also being about acquiring certain sets of skills. Multicultural skills refer to the capacity to work successfully across cultures, and to view the world with a particular emphasis on broadening one's cultural perspective on cross-cultural behaviour. It includes elements of curiosity, awareness of diversity and acceptance of complexity. We perceive the following skills, based on the work of Engelbrecht (1999), as useful within the context of project management across cultures in social work and social care.

Self-awareness

Self-awareness implies that you are striving for self-knowledge by being in touch with your own needs, motives and values. You attempt to be in control of your feelings and behaviour towards other cultures, are not easily intimidated by other cultures and are comfortable within your own culture. You should also be aware of personal unresolved cultural conflicts and make every attempt not to allow this to harm others. You should thus understand that you are a complex cultural being, no more or less worthy than project participants.

Communication

Communication across cultures should be both tactful and acceptable to various cultures. Your abilities to listen should be equally as good as your abilities to talk (also with people speaking other languages) and you must be aware of the effect your verbal and non-verbal communication (including appearance) has on others. You must be able to build professional relationships and networks and should possess effective negotiation skills. You should often communicate about the project's direction and objectives and accept that these will change frequently. You will furthermore make an effort to ensure that everybody understands the context of the project, their responsibilities and will take care in all communication. You are capable of repeating instructions several times in different ways, not only verbally, but also through pictures and sketches. Follow-up on communication is a given, as well as the assimilation and dissemination of information in a coherent way.

Empathic understanding

Not all people can enter into another person's experience with the same ease. Empathic understanding involves being able to think like someone else by separating yourself from your own frame of reference. This must, however, be an objective action. You should thus be mindful not only of yourself but also of others, in order to move between your own perspectives and those of project participants. You should furthermore bear in mind that habitual ways of thinking may be the result of cultural assumptions and not necessarily of personal pathology.

Openness to learning

You cannot be truly competent if you are not eager and open to learning. This implies an ambition to know more so as to manage more effectively, and is only achieved through self-development. Statements such as 'I work from experience' or 'I have an intuitive touch' may indicate an impediment to acquiring skills. You should thus be tuned into information gathering and analyses in order to uncover hidden cultural assumptions and become aware of how culture is shaping perceptions. This is the only way to start dialogue across cultural differences.

Assertiveness

It is important for you to act assertively within systems. This includes the manner in which you handle, express and assert yourself when dealing with participants of other cultural affiliations; and also your capacity to convey, for example, knowledge, values and skills in such a manner that the perceptions, rights and feelings of participants are respected. This does not imply passivity. You should thus be confident and creative in the employment of tools, techniques and strategies in the execution of processes, as different processes may have different meanings in diverse cultural contexts.

Optimism

In order to influence and motivate across cultures, you must believe in change and development and must be self-motivated. This can only be realized through a positive life-view. A project manager who revels in the negative aspects of life will have difficulty serving as an agent of growth, motivation and development for others. This involves an optimistic belief in the strengths and capabilities of project participants and the ability to convert deficits and obstacles into positive opportunities, and to see possibilities instead of limitations.

Adaptability

You ought to be able to adapt yourself according to changes and circumstances. This implies an easy transition from one situation to another and also quick adjustment to strange and different environments, a switching of styles and the accomplishment of tasks in more than one way. You should furthermore be able to deal with contradictions and paradoxes, shoulder dilemmas and take decisions without knowing the future and react constructively to unforeseen events.

Discretion

The nature of project management requires of you to continuously make judgements based on accurate and objective insights. This involves choices and decisions regarding ethical and legal issues, strategies, processes, etc. However, cultural descriptions should be limited to describing members of a cultural group as objectively as possible, and should not include an evaluative component, but provide an accurate description of beliefs, values and social norms.

Suggestions for the creation of a unique project culture through learning and development

Based on the above clarification of the need, meaning, implications and dimensions of project management across diverse cultures, it is evident that the biggest challenge for you is to create a unique project culture through an assessment of participants' cultural dimensions, learning and development. Our suggestions in terms of this challenge are the following:

- *Participatory management.* A participatory management style which has proved successful in project management across cultures should be promoted by you.

- *Cultural engagement.* You should create collective action in projects across cultures, as cultural understanding needs a collective response and all project participants should be on board. An ethos of cultural engagement with each other should be created in order to foster openness, eagerness and readiness to learn about cultural diversity and the implications thereof for the project.

- *Being a role model.* You should see learning and development in project management across cultures as continuous processes. Your actions speak louder than words and it is therefore important that you lead the way as role model.

- *Acknowledge potential in cultural differences.* A learning culture emphasizes the potential in cultural differences. To this end the strengths and capabilities of different cultures should be acknowledged; differences should not be perceived as deficits, although more work and perseverance could be required at times. Cultural clashes may be conducive to a fruitful understanding and negotiation of cultural differences. Differences are furthermore not inherently good or bad and should be translated by you to what works more effectively in specific contexts or where they may contribute to the attainment of specific project goals.

- *Allocate time to evaluate the impact of cultural dimensions on project performances.* In these events, project participants must reflect in a structured way on their cultural effectiveness, their understanding of the interplay of diverse cultures on the project, and their development of skills to contribute to the success of projects across diverse cultures.

- *Design strategies and tools.* Avoid abstract theorizing and quick-fix solutions for cultural differences. You must rather embark on a process of assessing practical and concrete experiences in order to identify options and to design strategies and tools, which should be evaluated and rectified after implementation. A learning cycle progressing from action, to reflection, to new thinking, to planning and then back to action should thus be employed.

It is important to deliberate upon how different cultural dimensions will impact on your role when managing projects in a globalized society. Therefore you should identify what essential skills you have at your disposal or need to acquire to maximize success, in order to create a unique project culture through learning and development. The 'On the Spot' activity in Box 9.2 will help you to do this.

Chapter summary

There is no one best way to manage across cultures. An overzealous and insensitive approach to convert project participants to change goals, strategies or behaviour may be counter-productive and can create resistance. To reduce complex cultural issues to simplistic formulas should also be avoided as well as colluding with rhetoric by using the right language and being politically correct without genuine action. Project management across diverse cultures in social work and social care is more than just a method, and you need not be an expert in cultural diversity. Project management across diverse cultures implies being open and taking up the challenge for the creation of a unique project culture through mutual learning and development. To work across diverse cultures requires sincerity – a disposition that is lived. Skills to manage projects successfully across diverse cultures should therefore become part of your identity.

Box 9.2

**'On the Spot' – Managing the cultural
dimensions of a project**

1. Using a project you have been involved in or one of the case
    studies in the book, identify specific cultural dimensions that
    may have an impact on projects.

2. Based on the identified cultural dimensions, what skills to
    manage across cultures should you develop in order to contribute
    to the success of this project?

3. What additional strategies and tools would you employ to
    promote a collective cultural understanding and to create a
    unique project culture that may contribute to the attainment of
    the project goals?

Action checklist

- Managing diversity in projects is important. Ensure that you have
  considered the opportunities that you may utilize to maximize the
  opportunities to be gained from this diversity.

- Identify the personal skills required for project managers to
  successfully manage projects across cultures.

References

Adams, S.L. and Anantatmula, V. (2010) 'Social and behavioural influences on team process.' *Project Management Journal 41*, 4, 89–98.

Assudani, R. and Kloppenborg, T.J. (2010) 'Managing stakeholders for project management success: an emergent model of stakeholders.' *Journal of General Management 35*, 3, Spring, 67–80.

Banks, S., Butcher, H., Henderson, P. and Robertson, J. (2003) *Managing Community Practice: Principles, Policies and Programmes.* Bristol: The Policy Press.

Barnardo's (2007) *Annual Report 2007.* Available at www.barnardos.org.uk/annual_report_and_accounts_2007.pdf, accessed on 22 November 2011.

Barnardo's (2010) *Annual Report and Accounts 2010.* Ilford: Barnardo's.

Berry, J.W. (1986) 'The Acculturation Process and Refugee Behaviour.' In C.L. Williams and J. Westermeyer (eds) *Refugee Mental Health in Resettlement Countries.* New York: Hemisphere.

Bond, M.H. and Smith, P.B. (1996) 'Cross-Cultural Social and Organizational Psychology.' *Annual Review of Psychology 1*, 47, 205–235.

Bourne, L. and Walker, D.H.T. (2004) 'Advancing project management in learning organisations.' *The Learning Organisation 11*, 3, 226–243.

Chapman, C. and Ward, S. (2002) 'Project Risk Management: The Required Transformations to Become Project Uncertainty Management.' In D.P. Slevin, D.I. Cleland and J.K. Pinto (eds) *The Frontiers of Project Management Research.* Newtown Square: Project Management Institute.

Charvat, J. (2003) *Project Management Methodologies: Selecting, Implementing and Supporting Methodologies and Processes for Projects.* New Jersey: John Wiley and Sons.

Chigona, W., Roode, D., Nabeel, N. and Pinnock, B. (2010) 'Investigating the impact of stakeholder management on the implementation of a public access project: the case of Smart Cape.' *South African Journal of Business Management 41*, 2, 39–49.

Clarke, N. (2006) 'Developing emotional intelligence through work-place learning: findings from a case study in healthcare.' *Human Resource Development International 9*, 447–465.

Clarke, N. (2010) 'Emotional intelligence and its relationship to transformational leadership and key project manager competencies.' *Project Management Journal 41*, 2, 5–20.

Clegg, S., Carter, C., Kornberger, M. and Schweitzer, J. (2011) *Strategy: Theory and Practice.* London: Sage.

Cooperrider, D.L., Whitney, D. and Stavros, J.M. (2005) *Appreciative Inquiry Handbook: The First in a Series of AI Workbooks for Leaders of Change.* San Francisco: Berrett-Koehler.

Danforth, E.J., Doying, A., Merceron, G. and Kennedy, L. (2010) 'Applying social science and public health methods to community-based pandemic planning.' *Journal of Business Continuity & Emergency Planning 4*, 4, 375–390.

Dartington-I (2006) *Common Language Training Pack: What is an Outcome?* Available at www.commonlanguage.org.uk/pages/lectures, accessed on 21 November 2011.

de Bono, E. (1987) *Six Thinking Hats.* London: Penguin.

Department for Education (DfE) (2010) *The Children Act 1989 Guidance and Regulations Volume 3: Planning Transition to Adulthood for Care Leavers Including the Care Leavers (England) Regulations 2010.* London: HMSO. Available at www.education.gov.uk/publications/standard/publicationDetail/Page1/DFE-00554-2010, accessed on 28 October 2011.

Department of Health (DoH) (2004) *Securing Good Health for the Whole Population – Final Report.* London: HMSO. Available at www.dh.gov.uk/en/Publicationsandstatistics/Publications/PublicationsPolicyAndGuidance/DH_4074426, accessed on 28 October 2011.

Department of Health (DoH) (2006) *Our Health, Our Care, Our Say: A New Direction for Community Services.* London: HMSO.

Department of Health (DoH) (2007a) *Independence, Choice and Risk: A Guide to Best Practice in Supported Decision Making.* London: HMSO. Available at www.dh.gov.uk/en/Publicationsandstatistics/ Publications/PublicationsPolicyAndGuidance/DH_074773, accessed on 28 October 2011.

Department of Health (DoH) (2007b) *World Class Commissioning: Vision.* London: HMSO. Available at www.dh.gov.uk/en/Publicationsandstatistics/Publications/PublicationsPolicyAndGuidance/ DH_080956, accessed on 28 October 2011.

Department of Health (DoH) (2008) *Dignity in Care: Becoming a Dignity Champion.* London: HMSO.

Department of Health (DoH) (2009a) *Living Well with Dementia: A National Dementia Strategy.* London: HMSO. Available at www.dh.gov.uk/en/Publicationsandstatistics/Publications/ PublicationsPolicyAndGuidance/DH_094058, accessed on 28 October 2011.

Department of Health (DoH) (2009b) *National Dementia Strategy Demonstrator Site.* Available at www. yhip.org.uk/silo/files/national-dementia-strategy-demonstrator-sites--executive-summary.doc, accessed on 28 October 2011.

Deresky, H. (2001) *International Management: Managing Across Borders and Cultures.* London: Prentice-Hall.

Ding, H. and Ding, X. (2008) 'Project management, critical praxis, and process-oriented approach to teamwork.' *Business Communication Quarterly 71,* 4, 456–471.

Dodgeson, M. and Rothwell, R. (1994) *The Handbook of Industrial Innovation.* Cheltenham: Edward Elgar.

Downey, M. (2003) *Effective Coaching: Lessons from the Coaches' Coach* (2nd edn). London: Texere.

Druskat, V. and Druskat, P. (2006) 'Applying Emotional Intelligence in Project Working.' In S. Pryke and H. Smyth (eds) *The Management of Complex Projects: A Relationship Approach.* Oxford: Blackwell.

Duggal, J.S. (2007) 'The Project, Program or Portfolio Office.' In J.R. Turner (ed.) *Gower Handbook of Project Management.* Aldershot: Gower Publishing.

Dulewicz, V. and Higgs, M.J. (2003) *Design of a New Instrument to Assess Leadership Dimensions and Styles.* Henley Working Paper 0311. Henley: Henley Management College.

Edmondson, A.C. and Nembhard, I.M. (2009) 'Product development and learning in project teams: the challenges are the benefits.' *The Journal of Product Innovation Management 26,* 123–138.

Elbeik, S. and Thomas, M. (1998) *Project Skills.* Oxford: Butterworth-Heinemann.

Engelbrecht, L.K. (1999) *Introduction to Social Work.* Wellington: Lanzo.

European Commission (2004) *Aid Delivery Methods Volume 1: Project Cycle Management Guidelines.* Brussels: European Commission.

Evans, S., Hills, S. and Orme, J. (2011) 'Doing more for less? Developing sustainable systems of social care in the context of climate change and public spending cuts.' *British Journal of Social Work.* First published online 23 July, 2011. doi:10.1093/bjsw/bcr108.

Freeman, R.E. (1984) *Strategic Management: A Stakeholder Approach.* Boston: Pitman.

Gallwey, T. (2000) *The Inner Game of Work.* London: Orion.

George, J.M. (1991) 'State or trait: effects of positive mood on prosocial behaviours at work.' *Journal of Applied Psychology 76,* 299–307.

Geraldi, J.G., Lee-Kelley, L. and Kutsch, E. (2010) 'The Titanic sunk, so what? Project manager response to unexpected events.' *International Journal of Project Management 28,* 6, 547–558.

Gilchrist, A. (2000) 'The well-connected community: networking to the "edge of chaos".' *Community Development Journal 35,* 3, 264–275.

Gouldner, A.W. (1957) 'Cosmopolitans and locals: toward an analysis of latent social roles.' *Administrative Science Quarterly 2,* 3, 281–306.

Graham, R.J. (1992) *A Survival Guide for the Accidental Project Manager.* Proceedings of the Project Management Institute Seminar/Symposium, Pittsburgh, PA.

Gray, C.F. and Larson, E.W. (2005) *Project Management* (3rd edn). London: McGraw-Hill.

Hafford-Letchfield, T. (2007) *Practising Quality Assurance in Social Care.* Exeter: Learning Matters.

Hafford-Letchfield, T. (2009) *Management and Organisations in Social Work.* Exeter: Learning Matters.

Hafford-Letchfield, T. (2010) *Social Care Management: Strategy and Business Planning.* London: Jessica Kingsley Publishers.

Hall, E.T. and Hall, M.R. (1990) *Understanding Cultural Differences.* Yarmouth: Intercultural Press.

Harris, J. and Unwin, P. (2009) 'Performance Management in Modernised Social Work.' In J. Harris and V. White (eds) *Modernising Social Work: Critical Considerations.* Bristol: Policy Press.

Harzing, A.W. and van Ruysseveldt J. (eds) (2004) *International Human Resource Management: An Integrated Approach* (2nd edn). London: Sage.

Her Majesty's Stationary Office (HMSO) (1998) *Crime and Disorder Act.* Available at www.legislation.gov. uk/ukpga/1998/37/contents, accessed on 28 October 2011.

Hofstede, G. (1980) *Culture's Consequences: International Differences in Work-Related Values.* London: Sage.

Hofstede, G. (2001) *Culture's Consequences: Comparing Values, Behaviours, Institutions, and Organizations across Nations* (2nd edn). Newbury Park, CA: Sage.

Hood, C. (1991) 'A public management for all seasons.' *Public Administration 69,* 3–19.

Horine, G.M. (2009) *Absolute Beginner's Guide to Project Management* (2nd edn). Indianapolis: Que Publishing.

House, R.J., Hanges, P.J., Javidan, M., Dorfman, W.P. and Gupta, V. (2004) *Culture, Leadership and Organization: The GLOBE Study of 62 Societies.* Thousand Oaks: Sage.

Ince, D. and Griffiths, A. (2010) *A Chronicling System for Children's Social Work: Learning from the ICS Failure.* Technical Report No. 2010/02. Milton Keynes: Open University. Available at http://computing-reports.open.ac.uk/2010/TR2010-02.pdf, accessed on 28 October 2011.

Jenkins, F. and Jones, R. (2007) 'Care Pathways and the Allied Health Professional.' In F. Jenkins and R. Jones (eds) *Key Topics in Healthcare Management: Understanding the Big Picture.* Oxford: Radcliffe Publishing.

Johnson, G., Scholes, K. and Whittington, R. (2005) *Exploring Corporate Strategy* (7th edn). Harlow: Pearson Education.

Kerzner, H. (2009) *Project Management: A Systems Approach to Planning, Scheduling and Controlling.* New Jersey: John Wiley and Sons.

Keys, B. and Case, T. (1990) 'How to become an influential manager.' *Academy of Management Executive 4,* 4, 38–51.

Kickert, W.J.M., Klijn, E.H. and Koppenjan, J.F.M. (eds) (1997) *Managing Complex Networks: Strategies for the Public Sector.* London: Sage.

Klijn, E., Edelenbos, J., Kort, M. and van Twist, M. (2008) 'Facing management choices: an analysis of managerial choices in 18 complex environmental public–private partnership projects.' *International Review of Administrative Sciences 74,* 2, 251–282.

Kloppenborg, T.J. (2009) *Contemporary Project Management.* Mason, OH: South-Western Cengage Learning.

Kluckhohn, F. and Strodtbeck, F. (1961) *Variations in Value Orientations.* Evanston: Peterson.

Koppenjan, J. and Klijn, E.H. (2004) *Managing Uncertainties in Networks: A Network Approach to Problem Solving and Decision Making.* London: Routledge.

Kroeber, A. and Kluckhohn, C. (1952) *Culture: A Critical Review of Concepts and Definitions.* Cambridge: Peabody Museum.

Laming, Lord (2009) *The Protection of Children in England: A Progress Report.* London: HMSO.

Latane, B., Williams, K. and Harkins, S. (1979) 'Many hands make light the work: the causes and consequences of social loafing.' *Journal of Personality and Social Psychology 37,* 822–832.

Lewin, K. (1947) 'Frontiers in group dynamics: concept, method and reality in social science; social equilibria and social change.' *Human Relations 1,* 5–41.

Li, Y.B. (2007) *Integrated Dynamic Perspective on Firm Competencies and Organisational Performance: A Study of China's Large SEOs*. PhD thesis, Dept of Real Estate and Construction, University of Hong Kong.

Marshall, R. and Hughes, R. (2008) 'Project management in nursing and residential care: an introduction.' *Nursing & Residential Care 10*, 11, 556–560.

Martin, V. (2002) *Managing Projects in Health and Social Care*. London: Routledge.

Mayer, J.D. and Salovey, P. (1997) 'What is Emotional Intelligence?' In P. Salovey and D. Sluyter (eds) *Educational Development and Emotional Intelligence: Educational Implications*. New York: Basic Books.

McElroy, B. and Mills, C. (2003) 'Managing Stakeholders.' In J.R. Turner (ed.) *People in Project Management*. Aldershot: Gower.

McKimm, J. and Phillips, K. (eds) (2009) *Leadership and Management in Integrated Services*. Exeter: Learning Matters.

Meier, S. (2008) 'Best project management and systems engineering practices in pre-acquisition practices in the federal intelligence and defense agencies.' *Project Management Journal 39*, 59–71.

Meredith, J.R. and Mantel, S.J. (2000) *Project Management: A Managerial Approach* (4th edn). New York: Wiley.

Miller, E., Whoriskey, M. and Cook, A. (2008) 'Outcomes for users and carers in the context of health and social care partnership working: from research to practice.' *Journal of Integrated Care 16*, 2, 21–28.

Mitchell, F., Dobson, C., McAlpine, A., Dumbreck, S., Wright, I. and Mackenzie, F. (2011) 'Intermediate care: lessons from a demonstrator project in Fife.' *Journal of Integrated Care 19*, 1, 26–36.

Moran, R.T., Harris, P.R. and Moran, S.V. (2007) *Managing Cultural Differences: Global Leadership Strategies for the 21st Century* (7th edn). Oxford: Butterworth-Heinemann.

Moriarty, P. and Buckley, F. (2003) 'Increasing team emotional intelligence through process.' *Journal of European Industrial Training 27*, 2, 98–110.

Munro, E. (2011) *The Munro Review of Child Protection: Final Report. A Child Centred System*. Department of Education. London: HMSO.

National Audit Office (NAO) (2009) *The National Offender Management Information*. London: HMSO.

National Audit Office (NAO) (2010) *Improving Dementia Services in England – An Interim Report*. London: HMSO.

National Audit Office (NAO) (2011a) *The National Programme for IT in the NHS: An Update on the Delivery of Detailed Care Records – Executive Summary*. London: HMSO.

National Audit Office (NAO) (2011b) *Lessons from PFI and Other Projects*. London: HMSO.

National Health Service (NHS) (2011) *Project Management Guide*. Available at www.institute.nhs.uk/ quality_and_service_improvement_tools/quality_and_service_improvement_tools/project_ management_guide.html, accessed on 28 October 2011.

Newell, S. and Swan, J. (2000) 'Trust and inter-organizational networking.' *Human Relations 53*, 10, 1287–1328.

Office of Government Commerce (OGC) (2005) *Common Causes of Project Failure*. London: OGC.

Office of Government Commerce (OGC) (2011) *PRINCE2*. Available at www.prince-officialsite.com, accessed on 17 January 2012.

Ofsted, Health Care Commission and HM Inspectorate of Constabulary (2008) *Joint Area Review – Haringey Children's Services Authority Area: Review of Services for Children and Young People, with Particular Reference to Safeguarding*. Available at www.education.gov.uk/publications/standard/ publicationDetail/Page1/HARINGEY-REVIEW, accessed on 28 October 2011.

Open University (2004) *Health and Social Services Management, Module 1 Managing Your Enterprise, Book 6*. Milton Keynes: Open University.

Parker, H. (2006) 'Managing People: The Dynamics of Teamwork.' In K. Walshe and J. Smith (eds) *Healthcare Management*. Maidenhead: OUP/McGraw-Hill Education.

Pedler, M., Burgoyne, J. and Boydell, T. (2007) *A Manager's Guide to Self Development* (5th edn). Maidenhead: McGraw-Hill.

Pender, S. (2001) 'Managing incomplete knowledge: why risk management is not sufficient.' *International Journal of Project Management 19*, 79–87.

Petch, A., Cook, A. and Miller, E. (2005) 'Focusing on outcomes: their role in partnership policy and practice.' *Journal of Integrated Care 13*, 6, 13–16.

Pinto, J.K. (2000) 'Understanding the role of politics in successful project management.' *International Journal of Project Management 18*, 85–91.

PRINCE2 (2011) Available at www.prince2.com/what-is-prince2.asp, accessed on 28 October 2011.

Rogers, E.M. (1995) *The Diffusion of Innovations* (3rd edn). New York: Free Press.

Rowlinson, S. and Cheung, Y.K.F. (2008) 'Stakeholder management through empowerment: modelling project success.' *Construction Management and Economics 26*, 611–623.

Sampson, E.E. (1999) *Dealing with Differences: An Introduction to the Social Psychology of Prejudice.* Orlando: Harcourt Brace.

Schwartz, S. (1992) 'Universals in the Content and Structure of Values: Theoretical Advances and Empirical Tests in 20 Countries.' In M. Zanna (ed.) *Advances in Experimental Social Psychology, Vol XXV.* New York: Academic Press.

Skills for Care (2002) *The National Occupational Standards for Social Work.* Available at www.skillsforcare. org.uk/developing_skills/National_Occupational_Standards/social_work_NOS.aspx, accessed on 28 October 2011.

Skills for Care (2004) *Leadership and Management: A Strategy for the Social Care Workforce.* Available at www.skillsforcare.org.uk/developing_skills/leadership_and_management/leadership_and_management_strategy.aspx, accessed on 21 November 2011.

Smale, G. (1998) *Managing Change through Innovation.* London: HMSO.

Smit, P.J. and Cronje, G.J. de J. (1999) *Management Principles: A Contemporary Edition for Africa* (2nd edn). Kenwyn: Juta & Co. Ltd.

Social Care Institute for Excellence (SCIE) (2004) *Involving Service Users and Carers in Social Work Education: SCIE Guide 4.* London: SCIE.

Social Care Institute for Excellence (SCIE) (2005) *Measuring Risk and Minimising Mistakes in Services to Children and Families.* London: SCIE.

Social Care Institute for Excellence (SCIE) (2006) *The Participation of Adult Service Users, Including Older People, in Developing Social Care: Guide 17.* London: SCIE.

Social Services Improvement Agency (SSIA) (2011) *Telecare Capital Grant & Telecare Revenue Grant.* Available at www.ssiacymru.org.uk/index.cfm?articleid=2214, accessed on 28 October 2011.

Social Work Inspection Agency (SWIA) (2006) *Performance Inspection of Social Work Services: Fife Council 2006.* Edinburgh: Scottish Executive.

Social Work Reform Board (2010) *Building a Safe and Confident Future: One Year On. Overarching Professional Standards for Social Workers in England.* Available at www.education.gov.uk/publications/eOrderingDownload/2%20Overarching%20professional%20standards.pdf, accessed on 28 October 2011.

Social Work Reform Board (2011) *Standards for Employers and Supervision Framework.* Available at www.education.gov.uk/swrb/a0074263/standards-for-employers-and-supervision-framework, accessed on 28 October 2011.

Sodowsky, G.R. and Plake, B.S. (1992) 'A study of acculturation differences among international people and suggestions for sensitivity to within-group differences.' *Journal of Counselling and Development 71*, 1, 53–59.

Spolander, G., Pullen-Sansfacon, A., Brown, M. and Engelbrecht, L. (2011) 'Social work education in Canada, England and South Africa: a critical comparison of undergraduate programmes.' *International Social Work.* First published online 31 January, 2011. doi:10.1177/0020872810389086.

Standards Australia and Standards New Zealand (2004) *AS/NZS 4360:2004 Risk Management.* Sydney, NSW: Standards Australia and Standards New Zealand.

Sunindijo, R.Y., Hadikusumo, B.H.W. and Ogunlana, S. (2007) 'Emotional intelligence and leadership styles in construction project management.' *Journal of Management in Engineering 23*, 4, 166–170.

Tayeb, M.H. (1996) *Management of a Multicultural Workforce.* New York: John Wiley and Sons.

Thane, P. (2009) *Memorandum Submitted to the House of Commons' Health Committee Inquiry: Social Care October 2009.* Available at www.historyandpolicy.org/docs/thane_social_care.pdf, accessed on 28 October 2011.

Thomas, M., Jacques, P.H., Adams, J.R. and Kihneman-Wooten, J. (2008) 'Developing an effective project: planning and team building combined.' *Project Management Journal 39*, 4, 105–113.

Trompenaars, F. and Hampden-Turner, C. (2004) *Managing People Across Cultures.* Oxford: Capstone.

Tuckman, B.W. (1965) 'Development sequence in small groups.' *Psychological Bulletin 63*, 384–399.

Turner, M. and Beresford, P. (2005) *Contributing on Equal Terms: Service User Involvement and the Benefits System: Adult Services Report 08.* London: SCIE.

Walker, D.H.S., Bourne, L. and Rowlinson, S. (2008) 'Stakeholders in the Supply Chain.' In D.H.S. Walker and S. Rowlinson (eds) *Procurement Systems: A Project Management Perspective.* Oxford: Taylor & Francis.

Waterman, R.H. Jr., Peters, T.J. and Philips, J.R. (1980) 'Structure is not organisation.' *Business Horizons*, June. Foundation for the School of Business, Indiana University.

Webb, S.A. (2006) *Social Work in a Risk Society: Social and Political Perspectives.* Basingstoke: Palgrave Macmillan.

West, M. and Markiewicz, L. (2004) *Creating Effective Teams: A Guide for Members and Leaders* (2nd edn). London: Sage.

Williams, P. (2002) 'The competent boundary spanner.' *Public Administration 80*, 1, 103–124.

Williams, T. and Samset, K. (2010) 'Issues in front-end decision making on projects.' *Project Management Journal*, April, 38–49.

Contributors

Lambert Engelbrecht is attached to the Department of Social Work at the University of Stellenbosch, South Africa. He has extensive experience as a social worker and is one of the leading researchers in the field of social work management and supervision in South Africa. Both his Masters and Doctoral studies were conducted in this field, and he has contributed widely to national and international publications and conferences on this topic. He has experience of a range of management positions in diverse contexts, and has a firmly recognized grounding in the design and teaching of management and supervision courses on undergraduate, post-graduate and continuous education level. Lambert inter alia serves as management consultant to a national social welfare organization and represents the South African social work academia on a national task team concerned with management and supervision.

Deborah Hadwin qualified as a social worker from Warwick University in 1999, and in 2000 her dissertation 'Well Matched' was published by the Social Care Association. 'Well Matched' considered to what extent children's needs remained a central concern in the process of identifying substitute family care. Deborah was employed as a social worker in a long-term children's team, then at a family centre for five years, where she completed her post-qualifying training and qualified as a practice assessor. Deborah has been an assistant team manager working in the area of unaccompanied asylum-seeking children for five years, the past three years in her current team.

Fiona Metcalfe is a registered social worker with experience in Children's Services as a practitioner and manager. She currently works in learning and development with responsibility for the continuous professional development of professional social work staff. She is particularly interested in exploring ways of supporting learning through sharing best practice and sees the development of communities of interest as an important element to promote critical and reflective thinking.

Claire Old is an experienced executive director in the NHS. As a nurse and midwife, she has moved through the system from the bottom up, having worked in every part of the NHS and in private and voluntary services, and having also, unusually for a nurse, run a general practice as a business manager for six years in the 'fundholding' era. Her social care experience comes from working as part of the Department of Health Change Agent Team and also from extensive experience of operationally managing joint teams and directing and managing joint commissioning teams. Her area of expertise is redesign and being able to personally lead not only what needs to be done, but creatively designing how we can do things better for patients.

Lorraine Stanforth qualified as a social worker in 1986. She works as a social care consultant and when writing the project management approach to Establishment Concerns was Interim Head of Safeguarding Adults at Enfield Council. She developed a Dignity Strategy for Enfield and latterly has worked on their Quality Assurance strategy in adult social care. She has also worked as a social researcher and has developed a number of audit tools to assist social work practitioners to identify gaps in practice and make improvements. Lorraine has a generic social work background, working across children and adult social care.

Rashida Suleman was born in 1968 in Nuneaton, Warwickshire. Further to her qualifications related to her roles, she is a mother of four children, one of whom has had mild learning difficulty, and has also been a carer for her mother-in-law for 21 years.

Rashida has also worked as a volunteer for five years for Guidepost Carers Support Service. She has been an active member for Untrap for seven years and has had involvement with Coventry University, Warwick University and the West Midlands Regional Office of the Open University. She has also worked with GSCC, which was a great experience for her, and she was on the carers' partnership board for three years at Warwick County Council. She is currently a Health Care Assistant for Coventry and Warwickshire Partnership Trust.

Colin Tysall was born in 1941 in Birmingham. At school he achieved five 'O' levels and post school further qualifications related to his professional roles. He is a father of three children and a grandfather. He has worked in a variety of industrial and professional roles including as an industrial radiographer, draughtsman, IT trainer associate, Mental Health Act manager, volunteer and service user advisor. As a result of a number of illnesses he has experience of a variety of social work, health and social care services.

Index